D0402890

HOWEVER LONG AND HARD THE ROAD

HOWEVER LONG AND HARD THE ROAD

JEFFREY R. HOLLAND

Deseret Book

Salt Lake City, Utah

© 1985 Deseret Book Company

All rights reserved. No part of this book may be reproduced in any
form or by any means without permission in writing from the publisher,
Deseret Book Company, P.O. Box 30178, Salt Lake City, Utah 84130.
This work is not an official publication of The Church of Jesus Christ of
Latter-day Saints. The views expressed herein are the responsibility
of the author and do not necessarily represent the position of the Church
or of Deseret Book Company.

Deseret Book is a registered trademark of Deseret Book Company.

First printing August 1985

Library of Congress Cataloging-in-Publication Data

Holland, Jeffrey R., 1940–
    However long and hard the road.

    Includes index.
    1. Christian life — Mormon authors — Addresses, essays,
lectures.   I. Title.
BX8656.H64   1985   284.4′89332   85-12945
ISBN 0-87747-625-X

Printed in the United States of America

10   9   8   7   6   5

For Mom and Dad, who believed
their children could do anything

Contents

Preface

The following pages come from a large stack of essays and addresses I have written over the past decade or so. They were, of course, not written—or spoken—to be published together, but they *do* have one thing in common. They are intended to be messages of hope. All of my professional life has been spent with young people, and universally they (like the rest of us) have needed support, encouragement, reassurance, and confidence. They have, in short, needed hope—that incentive to keep moving, keep trying, and keep believing until hope's sister virtues of faith and charity can also work their miracles. The thoughts contained in the pages that follow, including the invitation to repent when and where necessary, are shared with the intent that they might give encouragement to those who are struggling, that they might "succor the weak, lift up the hands which hang down, and strengthen the feeble knees."

1

For Times of Trouble

No one in mortality is spared the pain and sorrow and difficulty that are inevitable in a fallen world. We all have our share of troubles, and sometimes it may seem we have more than our share. But we must try to remember that our "afflictions shall be but a small moment," and if we "endure it well, God shall exalt [us] on high." Faithful Latter-day Saints in every generation should still sing with their pioneer ancestors— all is well, all is well.

We all ought to be concerned about a problem that is universal and that can, at any given hour, strike anyone anywhere. I believe it is a form of evil. At least I know it can have damaging effects that block our growth, dampen our spirits, diminish our hopes, and leave us vulnerable to other more conspicuous evils. I know of nothing that Satan uses quite so cunningly or cleverly in his work on a young man or woman. I speak of doubt (especially self-doubt), of discouragement, and of despair.

I don't wish to suggest that there aren't plenty of things in the world to be troubled about. In our lives individually and collectively, there surely are serious threats to our happiness. I watch an early morning news broadcast while I shave and then read a daily paper. That is enough to ruin anyone's day, and by then it's only 6:30 in the morning. Inflation, energy, jogging, mass murders, kidnappings, unemployment, floods. With all of this waiting for us, we are tempted, as W. C. Fields once said, to "smile first thing in the morning and get it over with." But my concerns are not the national and international ones. I would like to focus on those matters which do not make headlines in the *New York Times* but which may be quite important in our personal journals. I am anxious about the problems with our daily lives and loves and finances and futures; about our troubles concerning our place in the scheme of things and the value of our contribution; about our private fears regarding where we are going and whether we think we will ever get there.

I wish at the outset, however, to make a distinction that F. Scott Fitzgerald once made: "Trouble has no necessary connection with discouragement—discouragement has a germ of its own, as different from trouble as arthritis is different from a stiff joint." We all have troubles, but the "germ" of discouragement, to use Fitzgerald's word, is not in the trouble; it is in us—or to be more precise, I believe it is in Satan, the prince of darkness, the father of lies. And he would have it be in us. It's frequently a small germ, hardly worth going to a doctor for, but it will work and it will grow and it will spread. In fact, it can become almost a habit, a way of living and thinking, and there the greatest damage is done. Then it takes an increasingly severe toll on our spirit, for it erodes the deepest religious commitments we can make—those of faith, hope, and charity. We turn inward and look downward, and these greatest of Christlike virtues are damaged or at least impaired. We become unhappy and soon make others unhappy, and before long Lucifer laughs.

As with any other germ, a little preventive medicine ought to be practiced in terms of those things that get us down. There is a line from Dante that says, "The arrow seen before cometh less rudely." President John F. Kennedy put one aspect of the same thought into one of his state of the union messages this way: "The time to repair the roof is when the sun is shining." The Boy Scouts say it best of all: "Be prepared." That isn't just cracker-barrel wisdom with us; it is theology. "And angels shall fly through the midst of heaven, crying with a loud voice, . . . Prepare ye, prepare ye." (D&C 88:92.) "If ye are prepared ye shall not fear." (D&C 38:30.) Fear is part of what I wish to oppose. The scriptures teach that preparation—prevention, if you will—is perhaps the major weapon in our arsenal against discouragement and self-defeat.

Of course, some things are not under our control. Some disappointments come regardless of our effort and preparation, for God wishes us to be strong as well as good. We need to drive even these experiences into the corner, painful though they may be, and learn from them. In this too we have friends through the ages in whom we can take comfort and with whom we form timeless bonds.

Thomas Edison devoted ten years and all of his money to developing the nickel alkaline storage battery at a time when he was almost penniless. Through that period of time, his record and film production company was supporting the storage battery effort. Then one night the terrifying cry of "Fire!" echoed through the film plant. Spontaneous combustion had ignited some chemicals. Within moments all of the packing compounds, celluloids for records, film, and other flammable goods had gone up in flames. Fire companies from eight towns arrived, but the heat was so intense and the water pressure so low that the fire hoses had no effect. Edison was sixty-seven years old—no age to begin anew. His daughter was frantic, wondering if he was safe, if his spirit was broken, how he would handle a crisis such as this at his age. She saw him running toward her. He spoke first. He said, "Where's your mother? Go get her. Tell her to get her friends. They'll never see another fire like this as long as they live." At five-thirty the next morning, with the fire barely under control, he called his employees together and announced, "We're rebuilding." One man was told to lease all the machine shops in the area, another to obtain a wrecking crane from the Erie Railroad Company. Then, almost as an afterthought, Edison added, "Oh, by the way. Anybody know where we can get some money?"

Virtually everything we now recognize as a Thomas Edison contribution to our lives came *after* that disaster. Remember, "trouble has no necessary connection with discouragement— discouragement has a germ of its own."

To those who are trying hard and living right and things still seem burdensome and difficult, I say, take heart. Others have walked that way before you. Do you feel unpopular and different or outside the inside of things? Read Noah again. Go out there and take a few whacks on the side of your ark and see what popularity was like in 2500 B.C.

Does the wilderness stretch before you in a never-ending sequence of sand dunes? Read Moses again. Calculate the burden of fighting with the pharaohs and then a forty-year assignment in Sinai. Some tasks take time. Accept that. But as the scripture says, "They come to pass." They do end. We will cross over Jordan eventually. Others have done it—and so can we.

Are you afraid people don't like you? The Prophet Joseph Smith could share a few thoughts on that subject. Has health been a problem? Surely you will find comfort in the fact that a veritable Job has led the Church into one of the most exciting and revelatory decades of this entire dispensation. President Spencer W. Kimball has known few days in the past thirty years that have not been filled with pain or discomfort or disease. Is it wrong to wonder if President Kimball has in some sense become what he is not only *in spite* of the physical burdens but also in part *because* of them? You can take courage from your shared sacrifice with that giant of a man who has defied disease and death and who has shaken his fist at the forces of darkness and cried when there was hardly strength to

4

walk, "Oh, Lord, I am yet strong. Give me one more mountain." (See Joshua 14:11-12.)

Do you ever feel untalented or incapable or inferior? Would it help you to know that everyone else feels that way too, including the prophets of God? Moses initially resisted his destiny, pleading that he was not eloquent in language. Jeremiah thought himself a child and was afraid of the faces he would meet.

And Enoch? This is the young man who, when called to a seemingly impossible task, said, "Why is it that I have found favor in thy sight and am but a lad, and all the people hate me; for I am slow of speech; wherefore am I thy servant?" (Moses 6:31.) But Enoch was a believer. He stiffened his spine and squared his shoulders and went stutteringly on his way. Plain old ungifted, inferior Enoch. And this is what the angels would come to write of him: "So great was the faith of Enoch that he led the people of God, and their enemies came to battle against them; and he spake the word of the Lord, and the earth trembled, and the mountains fled, even according to his command; and the rivers of water were turned out of their course; and the roar of the lions was heard out of the wilderness; and all nations feared greatly, so powerful was the word of Enoch, and so great was the power of the language which God had given him." (Moses 7:13.)

Too little, too late, inadequate Enoch—whose name is now synonymous with transcendent righteousness! The next time you are tempted to paint your self-portrait dismal gray highlighted with lackluster beige, just remember that so have this kingdom's most splendid men and women been tempted. I say to you, as Joshua said to the tribes of Israel as they faced one of their most difficult tasks, "Sanctify yourselves: for tomorrow the Lord will do wonders among you." (Joshua 3:5.)

There is, of course, one source of despair more serious than all the rest, one that is linked with poor preparation of a far

5

more serious order. The opposite of sanctification, it is the most destructive discouragement in time or eternity. I speak of transgression against God. It is depression embedded in sin.

Here the most crucial challenge, once you recognize the seriousness of your mistakes, will be to believe that you can change, that there can be a different you. To disbelieve that is clearly a satanic device designed to discourage and defeat you. We ought to fall on our knees and thank our Father in heaven that we belong to a church and have grasped a gospel that promises repentance to those who will pay the price. Repentance is not a foreboding word. It is, after faith, the most encouraging word in the Christian vocabulary. Repentance is simply the scriptural invitation for growth and improvement and progress and renewal. You can change! You can be anything you want to be in righteousness.

If there is one lament I cannot abide, it is the poor, pitiful, withered cry, "Well, that's just the way I am." If you want to talk about discouragement, that is one that discourages me. I've heard it from too many people who want to sin and call it psychology. And I use the word *sin* to cover a vast range of habits, some seemingly innocent enough, that nevertheless bring discouragement and doubt and despair.

You can change anything you want to change, and you can do it very fast. Another satanic suckerpunch is that it takes years and years and eons of eternity to repent. That's just not true. It takes exactly as long to repent as it takes you to say, "I'll change"—and mean it. Of course there will be problems to work out and restitutions to make. You may well spend—indeed, you had better spend—the rest of your life proving your repentance by its permanence. But change, growth, renewal, and repentance can come for you as instantaneously as they did for Alma and the sons of Mosiah. Even if you have serious amends to make, it is not likely that you would qualify for the term "the vilest of sinners," which is the phrase Mormon used in describing these young men. Yet as Alma recounts his own experience, it appears to have been as instantaneous as it was stunning. (See Alma 36.)

Do not misunderstand. Repentance is not easy or painless or convenient. It is a bitter cup from hell. But only Satan, who dwells there, would have you think that a necessary and required acknowledgment is more distasteful than permanent residence. Only he would say, "You can't change. You won't change. It's too long and too hard to change. Give up. Give in. Don't repent. You are just the way you are." That is a lie born of desperation. Don't fall for it.

The Brethren used to announce at general conference the names of those who had been called on missions. Not only was this the way friends and neighbors learned of the call, but more often than not it was the way the missionary learned of it as well. One such prospect was Eli H. Pierce. A railroad man by trade, he had not been very faithful in the Church, "even had my inclinations led in that direction, which I frankly confess they did not," he admitted. His mind had been given totally to what he demurely called "temporalities." He said he had never read more than a few pages of scripture in his life, that he had spoken at only one public gathering (an effort that he says "was no credit" to himself or those who heard him), and he used the vernacular of the railroad and barroom with a finesse born of long practice. He bought cigars wholesale—a thousand at a time—and he regularly lost his paycheck playing pool. Then this classic understatement: "Nature never endowed me with a superabundance of religious sentiment; my spirituality was not high and probably even a little below average."

Well, the Lord knew what Eli Pierce was and he knew something else. He knew what Eli Pierce could become. When the call came that October 5, 1875, Eli wasn't even in the Tabernacle. He was out working on one of the railroad lines. A fellow employee, once he had recovered from the shock of it all, ran out to telegraph the startling news. Brother Pierce writes: "At the very moment this intelligence was being flashed

7

over the wires, I was sitting lazily thrown back in an office rocking chair, my feet on the desk, reading a novel and simultaneously sucking on an old Dutch pipe just to vary the monotony of cigar smoking. As soon as I had been informed of what had taken place, I threw the novel in the waste basket, the pipe in the corner (and have never touched either to this hour). I sent in my resignation . . . to take effect at once, in order that I might have time for study and preparation. I then started into town to buy [scripture]."

Then Eli wrote these stirring words: "Remarkable as it may seem, and has since appeared to me, a thought of disregarding the call, or of refusing to comply with the requirement, never once entered my mind. The only question I asked—and I asked it a thousand times—was: 'How can I accomplish this mission? How can I, who am so shamefully ignorant and untaught in doctrine, do honor to God and justice to the souls of men, and merit the trust reposed in me by the Priesthood?'"

With such genuine humility fostering resolution rather than defeating it, Eli Pierce fulfilled a remarkable mission. His journal could appropriately close on a completely renovated life with this one line: "Throughout our entire mission we were greatly blessed." But I add one experience to make the point.

During the course of his missionary service, Brother Pierce was called in to administer to the infant child of a branch president whom he knew and loved. Unfortunately the wife of the branch president had become embittered and now seriously objected to any religious activity within the home, including a blessing for this dying child. With the mother refusing to leave the bedside and the child too ill to move, the humble branch president with his missionary friend Eli retired to a small upper room in the house to pray for the baby's life. The mother, suspecting just such an act, sent one of the older children to observe and report back.

There in that secluded chamber the two men knelt and prayed fervently until, in Brother Pierce's own words, "we felt that the child would live and knew that our prayers had been heard." Arising from their knees, they turned slowly only to see the young girl standing in the partially open doorway gazing intently into the room. She seemed, however, quite oblivious to the movements of the two men. She stood entranced for some seconds, her eyes immovable. Then she said, "Papa, who was that man in there?" Her father said, "That is Brother Pierce. You know him." "No," she said matter-of-factly, "I mean the *other* man." "There was no other, darling, except Brother Pierce and myself. We were praying for the baby." "Oh, there was another man," the child insisted, "for I saw him standing [above] you and Brother Pierce and he was dressed in white." Now if God in his heavens will do that for a repentant old cigar-smoking, inactive, stern-swearing pool player, don't you think he'll do it for you? He will if your resolve is as deep and permanent as Eli Pierce's. In the Church we ask for faith, not infallibility. Here are five things to remember when trouble strikes. They are among the most fundamental truths of a gospel-centered life.

1. Pray earnestly and fast with purpose and devotion. Some difficulties, like devils, do not come out save by fasting and by prayer. Ask in righteousness and you shall receive. Knock with conviction and it shall be opened unto you.

2. Immerse yourself in the scriptures. You will find your own experiences described there. You will find spirit and strength there. You will find solutions and counsel. Nephi says, "The words of Christ will tell you all things what you should do." (2 Nephi 32:3.)

3. Serve others. The heavenly paradox is that only in so doing can you save yourself.

4. Be patient. As Robert Frost said, with many things the only way out is through. Keep moving. Keep trying.

5. Have faith. "Has the day of miracles ceased? Or have angels ceased to appear unto the children of men? Or has he withheld the power of the Holy Ghost from them? Or will he,

so long as time shall last, or the earth shall stand, or there shall be one man upon the face thereof to be saved? Behold I say unto you, Nay; for it is by faith that miracles are wrought; and it is by faith that angels appear and minister unto men." (Moroni 7:35-37.)

I heard the story once of a young man who left a small western town to travel east. The details of the story I have probably missed, but the personal impact the message had upon me is still reverberating. He had never traveled much beyond his little hometown and certainly had never ridden a train. But his older sister and brother-in-law needed him under some special circumstances, so his parents agreed to free him from the farm work in order to go. They drove him to Salt Lake City and put him on the train—new Levi's, not-so-new boots, very frightened, and eighteen years old.

There was one major problem and it terrified him. He had to change trains in Chicago. Furthermore, it involved an overnight layover, and that was a fate worse than death. His sister had written and carefully outlined when the incoming train would arrive and how and where and when he was to catch the outgoing line, but he was terrified.

And then the young man's humble, plain, sun-scarred father did something no one should ever forget. He said, "Son, wherever you go in this church there will always be somebody to stand by you. That's part of what it means to be a Latter-day Saint." He stuffed into the pocket of his son's calico shirt the name of a bishop he had taken the time to identify from sources at Church headquarters. If the boy had troubles or became discouraged and afraid, he was to call the bishop and ask for help.

Well, the train ride progressed rather uneventfully until the train pulled into Chicago. And even then the young man did pretty well at collecting his luggage and making it to the nearby hotel room that had been reserved for him by his brother-in-law. But then the clock began to tick and night began to fall, and faith began to fail. Could he find his way back to the station? Could he find the right track and train? What if it was late? What if he was late? What if he lost his ticket? What if his sister had made a mistake and he ended up in New York? What if? What if? What if?

Without those well-worn boots ever hitting the floor, that big raw-boned boy flew across the room, nearly pulled the telephone out of the wall, and, fighting back tears and troubles, called the bishop. Alas, the bishop was not home, but the bishop's wife was. She spoke long enough to reassure him that absolutely nothing could go wrong that night. He was, after all, safe in the room, and what he needed more than anything else was a night's rest. Then she said, "If tomorrow morning you are still concerned, follow these directions and you can be with our family and other ward members until train time. We will make sure you get safely on your way." She carefully spelled out the directions, had him repeat them back, and suggested a time for him to come.

With slightly more peace in his heart, he knelt by his bed as he had every night of his eighteen years and then waited for morning to come. Somewhere in the night the hustle and bustle of Chicago in the 1930s subsided into peaceful sleep.

At the appointed hour the next morning he set out. A long walk, then catch a bus. Then transfer to another. Watch for the stop. Walk a block, change sides of the street, and then one last bus. Count the streets carefully. Two more to go. One more to go. I'm here. Let me out of this bus. It worked, just as she said.

Then his world crumbled before his very eyes. He stepped out of the bus onto the longest stretch of shrubbery and grass he had ever seen in his life. She had said something about a park, but he thought a park was a dusty acre in a western town with a netless tennis court in one corner. Here he stood looking at the vast expanse of Lincoln Park with not a single friendly face in sight.

There was *no* sign of a bishop or a meetinghouse. And the bus was gone. It struck him that he had no idea where he was or what combination of connections with who knows what number of buses would be necessary to get him back to the station. Suddenly he felt more alone and overwhelmed than at any moment in his life. As the tears welled up in his eyes, he despised himself for feeling so afraid—but he was, and the tears would not stop. He stepped off the sidewalk away from the bus stop into the edge of the park. He needed some privacy for his tears, as only an eighteen-year-old could fully appreciate. But as he stepped away from the noise, fighting to control his emotions, he thought he heard something hauntingly familiar in the distance. He moved cautiously in the direction of the sound. First he walked, and then he walked quickly. The sound was stronger and firmer and certainly it was familiar. Then he started to smile, a smile that erupted into an audible laugh, and then he started to run. He wasn't sure that was the most dignified thing for a newcomer to Chicago to do, but this was no time for dignity. He ran, and he ran fast. He ran as fast as those cowboy boots could carry him—over shrubs, through trees, around the edge of a pool.

> Though hard to you this journey may appear,
> Grace shall be as your day.

The sounds were crystal clear and he was weeping newer, different tears. For there over a little rise huddled around a few picnic tables and bundles of food were the bishop and his wife and their children and most of the families of that little ward. The date: July 24. The sound: A slightly off-key, a cappella rendition of lines that any LDS boy could recognize.

> Gird up your loins; fresh courage take;
> Our God will never us forsake;
> And soon we'll have this tale to tell—
> All is well! all is well!

It was Pioneer Day. The gathering to which he had been invited was a 24th of July celebration. Knowing that it was about time for the youth to arrive, the ward members had thought it a simple matter to sing a verse or two of "Come, Come, Ye Saints" to let him know their location.

Elisha, with a power known only to the prophets, had counseled the king of Israel on how and where and when to defend against the warring Syrians. The king of Syria, of course, wished to rid his armies of this prophetic problem. "Therefore sent he thither horses, and chariots, and a great host: and they came by night, and compassed the city round about. . . . They compassed the city both with horses and chariots."

If Elisha was looking for a good time to be depressed, this was it. His only ally was the president of the local teachers quorum. It was one prophet and one lad against the world. And the boy was petrified. He saw the enemy everywhere—difficulty and despair and problems and burdens everywhere. With faltering faith Elisha's youthful companion cried, "Alas, my master! how shall we do?" And Elisha's reply? "Fear not: for they that be with us are more than they that be with them."

"They that be with us?" Now, faith is fine and courage wonderful, but this is ridiculous, the boy thought. There were no others with them. He could recognize a Syrian army when he saw one, and he knew that one child and an old man were not strong odds against it. But Elisha's promise was: "Fear not: for they that be with us are more than they that be with them." Then Elisha turned heavenward, saying, "Lord, I pray thee, open his eyes, that he may see." And, we are told, "the Lord opened the eyes of the young man; and he saw: and, behold, the mountain was full of horses and chariots of fire round about Elisha." (2 Kings 6:14-17.)

In the gospel of Jesus Christ we have help from both sides of the veil. When disappointment and discouragement strike—and they will—we need to remember that if our eyes could be opened, we would see horses and chariots of fire as far as the eye can see, riding at great speed to come to our protection. They will always be there, these armies of heaven, in defense of Abraham's seed. We have been given this promise from heaven:

"Ye are little children, and ye have not as yet understood how great blessings the Father hath in his own hands and prepared for you; and ye cannot bear all things now; nevertheless, be of good cheer, for I will lead you along." (D&C 78:17-18.) "I will go before your face. I will be on your right hand and on your left, . . . and mine angels [shall be] round about you, to bear you up." (D&C 84:88.) "The kingdom is yours and the blessings thereof are yours, and the riches of eternity are yours." (D&C 78:18.)

Yes, "we'll find the place which God for us prepared." And on the way,

> We'll make the air with music ring,
> Shout praises to our God and King;
> Above the rest these words we'll tell—
> All is well! all is well!

2

"Whom Say Ye That I Am?"

In times of extreme difficulty, the only strength upon which we can fully rely is Jesus Christ, the Savior of the world. Indeed, any tribulation will be considered well worth it if it humbles us, increases our faith, and brings us closer to Him who bought us with his own pain and blood. In the depths of despair we may find ourselves coming to know him in a completely new way, finding that he goes before us on our right hand and on our left, that his spirit is in our hearts, and that his angels are round about us to bear us up.

To the Lord's covenant people, names—particularly proper names—have always been very important. Adam and Eve themselves bore names that suggested their roles here in mortality (Moses 1:34; 4:26), and, when important covenants were made, men like Abram and Jacob took on new names that signaled a new life as well as a new identity (Genesis 17:5; 32:28).

Because of this reverence for titles and the meanings they conveyed, the name Jehovah, sometimes transliterated as *Yahweh*, was virtually unspoken among that people. This was the unutterable name of Deity, that power by which oaths were sealed, battles won, miracles witnessed. Traditionally, he was identified only through a tetragrammaton, four Hebrew letters variously represented in our alphabet as *IHVH, JHVH, JHWH, YHVH, YHWH.*

Since those early days of the Hebrews, others have thought the attempt to know the Lord God of Israel by naming him was both irreverent and impossible. St. Augustine kept warning his colleagues, *"Melius scitur Deus nesciendo"*—"God is better known by not knowing." (*De Ordine.*) And Pierre in Leo Tolstoy's *War and Peace* (Book 6) scribbled in his diary against those religioscientists who would "dissect everything to comprehend it and kill everything to examine it." These two might have formed a highly unlikely trio with Goethe's *Faust* to say:

> Who dare name Him? . . .
> Name it Happiness! Heart! Love! God!
> I have no name for that!
> Feeling is all in all;
> Name is but sound and smoke,
> Beclouding Heaven's glow. (*Faust,* Part 1.)

In fact, name is not sound and smoke, but rather one method, given of our Father, by which we try to know better the great Jehovah, the Lord Jesus Christ. Even while granting that there is one sense in which "feeling is all in all," we know that somehow "happiness, heart, love" are not enough to describe the living son of the living God. Those are abstractions, and he is clearly the least abstract being in our lives. So, while we must be fully aware of the limitations—in our lives, in our language, in our ability to comprehend or appreciate—we still do well to praise Deity by name and in some small way come to know him better by what he says he is. Men should be aware, and beware, "how they take my name in their lips." (D&C 63:61.)

To John on the Isle of Patmos, the resurrected Jesus announced himself, "I am Alpha and Omega, the beginning and the ending, . . . which is, and which was, and which is to come, the Almighty." (Revelation 1:8.) Nothing is so pervasive in our lives, nothing so encompassing and enfolding and upholding, as the Savior of this world and the Redeemer of all men. Alpha, the first letter of the Greek alphabet, suggests commencement and inception. "I was in the beginning with the Father," he reveals (D&C 93:21), and, as the Firstborn, he stood at the right hand of the Father in the councils of heaven and in the work of creation. It was by our unity with him (as he was one with the Father) that we survived a great conflict between good and evil before this world was created. By the "blood of the Lamb, and by the word of [our] testimony," we overcame the opposition of Satan, "that old serpent, called the Devil" (Revelation 12:7-11), and we saw him cast out into the earth ahead of us. Reaching back in time to scenes untouched by memory but still resonant in our souls, we realize that even then we recognized the role of one who, as both friend and brother, would pave for us the narrow path of perfection. However little we know of our premortal state, we know that this beloved Son of God strengthened our convictions and created this world to which we would come. He was "the firstborn of every creature." (Colossians 1:15.)

I am Alpha.

As he was in the beginning, so will he be when this world ends. As Omega, a name taken from the last letter of the Greek alphabet, Christ is the terminus, the end cause as well as the end result of mortal experience. At his coming we will know what we might have become. John wrote, "Now are we the sons of God, and it doth not yet appear what we shall be: but we know that, when he shall appear, we shall be like him; for we shall see him as he is." (1 John 3:2.)

We hope we will be very much like him—not in sovereignty or station or degree of sacrifice, but perhaps in some portion of virtue and love and obedience. He will come to reign as the Messiah, Lord of lords and King of kings, and we will call him Master. In this finality, which is for the redeemed a beginning, the Lord of this earth will come, in Solomon's language, as "fair as the moon, clear as the sun, and terrible as an army with banners." (Song of Solomon 6:10.)

I am Omega.

These letters from the Greek suggest the universal role of Jesus from the beginning of the world to its end. But he ought to be Alpha and Omega in the particular as well—*our* personal beginning and *our* individual end, that model by which we shape our journey of threescore years and ten, and the standard by which we measure it at its conclusion.

In every choice we make, he ought to be our point of reckoning, our charted course, our only harbor ahead. He should be for us individually what he is for all men collectively—the very brackets of existence, the compass of our privilege. We should not stray outside him. We should not want to try.

I am Alpha and Omega.

In addition to, and (to the extent it can be) more important than, Jesus' past and future life is his eternal presence. That is, Christ is not only Alpha *and* Omega, he is Alpha *through* Omega—complete, abiding, permanent, unchanged. As well as being before and after us, Christ will, if we choose, be with us.

The great challenge of our lives is usually not meditating on what we once were or wishing on what we may yet become, but rather living in the present moment as God would have us live. Fortunately, Christ can be in that moment for each of us since "all things are present" before him (D&C 38:2) and "time only is measured unto men" (Alma 40:8).

To Moses, who was faced not with a dimming past or a misty future nearly so much as with the brutal presence of a godless Pharaoh, Jehovah said, "I AM THAT I AM. . . . Say unto the children of Israel, I AM. . . . This is my name for ever." (Exodus 3:14-15.) Repentance and faith, service and compassion—now is always the right time for these. The past is to be learned from, not lived in, and the future is to be planned for, not paralyzed by. God has declared himself in the present tense.

I am the Great I AM.

Such a journey from beginning through present to end suggests a path, a course of travel, and Jesus said he was "the Way." He did not say he would show the way (although he did): he said he *was* the way. (John 14:6.) To travel here suggests something more than merely knowing the terrain, watching for pitfalls, and setting out at a brisk pace. It means all of that plus the sobering admission that we will need his merciful assistance for every step of the journey.

This particular way is impassable alone. He waits patiently for us while we rest. He encourages us when we murmur. He calls us back when we stray. Ultimately, he carries us on his shoulders, rejoicing, because we find the heights are too great and the waters too deep. (See Luke 15:5.) Only strict adherence—adherence in its most literal sense—to the Lord Jesus Christ will see us through, for there is "none other name under heaven given among men, whereby we must be saved." (Acts 4:12.)

Using the metaphor of the sheepfold, he told his disciples, "I am the door: by me if any man enter in, he shall be saved." (John 10:9.) Thus, the place the way leads to is not only inevitable by, but also in a sense incidental to, the way itself. "No man cometh unto the Father, but by me," Jesus warned. (John 14:6.)

It is little wonder that Nephi closed his record and his life with the stirring injunction to follow undeviatingly the straight and narrow path once it is, through the grace of God, begun. "Ye must press forward with a steadfastness in Christ, having a perfect brightness of hope, and a love of God and of all men. . . . My beloved brethren, this is the way; and there is none other way. . . . Feast upon the words of Christ; for behold, the words of Christ will tell you all things what ye should do." (2 Nephi 31:20-21; 32:3.)

I am the Way.

In our dispensation the Lord has defined truth as "knowledge of things as they are, and as they were, and as they are to come." (D&C 93:24.) To his disciples in the meridian of time he said, "If ye continue in my word, then are ye my disciples indeed; and ye shall know the truth, and the truth shall make you free." (John 8:31-32.) The prescribed method for coming to knowledge (and subsequent freedom) is to "give diligent heed to the words of eternal life" (D&C 84:43), yet many of us spend precious little time with those words.

A monastic study of the gospel is not intended, for we are to be "doers of the word, and not hearers only." (James 1:22.) But many of us neither hear nor do. Furthermore, it is both reasonable and revealed that there is a dialectical link between learning the word of the Lord and coming to the Word, which is the Lord. (D&C 84:45-47; John 1:1-14.) On one occasion Jesus said the latter-day members of his church were under condemnation because they had treated lightly the things they had received, "even the Book of Mormon and the former commandments which I have given." (D&C 84:54-57.) Like the world that groans under the bondage of sin and ignorance, we will be bound and burdened until we know the words of truth and salvation.

We can never get far from the revealed fact that it is impossible for a man to be saved in ignorance and that the person who has diligently gained more knowledge and intelligence (i.e., truth) in this life will have great advantages in the world to come. (D&C 131:6; 130:19.) To study the scriptures, to obey the living prophets, to pray and meditate upon the truths of the gospel—in short, to know things as they really are— these will lead us to freedom. "If ye abide in me, and my words abide in you, ye shall ask what ye will, and it shall be done unto you." (John 15:7.)

I am the Truth.

Death and hell in their most extreme extensions have been referred to as outer darkness. (See D&C 101:91.) On the other hand, eternal life and the degrees of glory are sometimes scripturally described by metaphors of light and vision. When God first looked out upon the earth, it was "without form, and void; and darkness was upon the face of the deep." The fundamental need was obvious, and he said, "Let there be light." (Genesis 1:2-3.)

Later, Jesus would say, "I am the light of the world: he that followeth me shall not walk in darkness, but shall have the light of life." (John 8:12.) Christ is, according to our revelations, the light of the sun, the light of the moon, the light of the stars and of the earth. Furthermore, he is the light which "giveth you light, . . . [which] enlighteneth your eyes, which is the same light that quickeneth your understandings." (D&C 88:7-11.)

Light, like truth, forsakes the evil one, that prince of darkness who was cast out of heaven into the earth. The casualty of that rebellious son's fall is glimpsed at least partially in the meaning of his name Lucifer, literally "a bearer of light," a son of the morning. Having lost that fresh radiance of an eternal dawn and destined to dwell in a kingdom without glory (i.e., light), Satan now consciously seeks to take away light from the children of men. We are able to elude such lifeless desolation, however, because God once again looked upon a darkened world and said, "Let there be light." He gave his Only Begotten Son that whosoever would believe in him should not perish, but have everlasting life. (John 3:16.)

I am the Light and the Life of the world.

If in times of trial we wander, we need someone wise and concerned to give aid. To those, Jesus said he was the Good

Shepherd, one who would leave the ninety and nine safely enfolded to rescue the lamb that is lost. And this shepherd is not a hireling, one who trembles at the sound of a wolf and flees at the sight of thieves. Ownership of the flock makes a great deal of difference, and this watchman will protect at the very cost of his life. "I . . . know my sheep," he promised, "and I lay down my life for the sheep." (John 10:14-15.)

Safely returned, we again graze along, not knowing what the loss of our life might have been like. With staff in hand, Christ must often muse lovingly over such youthful artlessness. "Verily, verily, I say unto you, ye are little children, and ye have not as yet understood how great blessings the Father hath in his own hands and prepared for you; and ye cannot bear all things now; nevertheless, be of good cheer, for I will lead you along. The kingdom is yours and the blessings thereof are yours, and the riches of eternity are yours." (D&C 78:17-18.)

I am the Good Shepherd.

Of course, by paradox, this Shepherd was also a lamb—the Lamb of God. From Adam to the atonement of Christ, men were commanded to offer the firstlings of their flocks, that purest lamb without spot or blemish, as a similitude of the sacrifice that God the Father would make of his Firstborn, his Only Begotten Son, who lived with perfection in the midst of imperfection. As they met for the Passover meal to commemorate the preservation of the firstborn of their fathers, Jesus taught his disciples that the blood of the lamb was once again to save them from destruction. In the hours that then followed, Jesus offered both body and blood that all who would might come cleansed unto the Father, having washed white their robes in the blood of the Lamb. (Luke 22:17-20; Exodus 12:2-10; Revelation 7:14.)

In some way that is to our minds incomprehensible and beyond the deepest appreciation of our hearts, Jesus Christ took upon himself the burden of men's sins from Adam to the end of the world. Before he was born into this mortal world, it was prophesied of him, "He was oppressed, and he was afflicted, yet he opened not his mouth: he is brought as a lamb to the slaughter, and as a sheep before her shearers is dumb, so he openeth not his mouth. He was taken from prison and from judgment: and who shall declare his generation? for he was cut off out of the land of the living: for the transgression of my people was he stricken." (Isaiah 53:7-8.)

I am the Lamb of God.

The promise of this pursuit—seeking truth, following light, building on certainty; in short, living the gospel of Christ—is peace in this world as well as eternal life in the world to come. (D&C 59:23.) Peace is, unfortunately, a commodity that is little known to this world. Nations battle against nations, fathers are at war with their sons, conflicts rage within the individual soul.

But if we will, the "Sun of righteousness" may rise over such dark scenes "with healing in his wings." (Malachi 4:2.) Then peace, the only real peace we know, is indeed a reality with man.

The Latin term is *pax*, literally "an agreement." Agreement!—agreement with him who has made agreement for us. Only then can the destruction of body and soul cease, not simply in armistice but victory. "Sue for peace, not only to the people that have smitten you, but also to all people." (D&C 105:38.) The worlds in and outside a man's heart cry out for harmony and agreement.

I am the Prince of Peace.

Jehovah said to the prophet Isaiah that in building the kingdom of God on earth, a "stone, a tried stone, a precious corner stone, a sure foundation" would be used. (Isaiah 28:16.) He was, of course, speaking of himself. Paul used that same imagery in declaring that Jesus was the chief cornerstone, that basic block around which a foundation of apostles and prophets would be laid and onto which the Church of God would be built. (Ephesians 2:20.) Peter noted that builders of lesser vision simply shoved him aside in favor of less substantial material. (See Acts 4:11.) The tragic irony is that to most, he was not a building stone at all, but rather a mere stumbling block, a huge boulder obstructing the journey toward death. (See 1 Corinthians 1:23.)

We must be wiser than this. Helaman pleaded with his sons as prophets and patriarchs plead today: "Remember, remember that it is upon the rock of our Redeemer, who is Christ, the Son of God, that ye must build your foundation; that when the devil shall send forth his mighty winds, yea, his shafts in the whirlwind; yea, when all his hail and his mighty storm shall beat upon you, it shall have no power over you to drag you down to the gulf of misery and endless wo, because of the rock upon which ye are built, which is a sure foundation, a foundation whereon if men build they cannot fall." (Helaman 5:12.) Everyone will be tempered and tried. The sun will rise on the evil as well as the good, and the rains will descend on the just as well as the unjust. (Matthew 5:45.) But a life built on a firm foundation will endure.

I am the Stone of Israel.

The life of Christ is a precious jewel that flashes in the flame of the sunlight and blinds our eyes with its rays. The prophets have, in reverence and holy appreciation, sought to speak of it, to praise him for the love and glory he displays. Some of the titles we hear often—Savior, Redeemer, Messiah; others we recognize less well—Dayspring, Ahman, Bishop of Our Souls. He is the Mediator, the Advocate, the Author and Finisher of our Faith. He is Wonderful, Counselor, the Mighty God, the Everlasting Father. He is the Holiest of All, the Lion of Judah, the Mighty One of Jacob. He is the Man of Sorrows, the Horn of Salvation. He is Eternal and Everlasting. He is the Son of Man. He is the Bright and Morning Star. The list is only representative of another list that is only representative. What he is goes on forever, flashing in the sun.

We once called upon a member of our stake to bear her testimony in stake conference. She told of losing her four-year-old son in a large metropolitan department store. She looked frantically up and down every aisle, her heart beating faster and faster at every disappointing turn. She asked the store personnel to assist her, and she even ran into the street to see if he had left the building. She kept reassuring herself that everything was all right, that he couldn't be far, that surely he was safe. But minutes turned into dozens of minutes, and she could not find her son.

"I started to cry," she told us. "I started to cry and wanted to run up to the people shopping in that store and grab them and shake them until they understood. 'My boy is lost!' I wanted to scream. 'How can you stand there and worry about shirts and slips and pocketbooks? Don't you understand? *My boy is lost!*'"

In the midst of that panic and despair she had a moment of revelation. She immediately took the escalator to the tenth—and last—floor of the building. There, at the top of the stairs, was Darren, not knowing quite how to get an "up" escalator to take him back down to his mother.

"I'm sure glad you came, Mom," he said, a bit shaken. "I think I was in real trouble." My friend said that there on her knees, with her arms "unfailing 'round" her son, she saw through her tears a bright new meaning in the redemptive pain of the Lord Jesus Christ, paid for loved ones who were lost.

"Whom say ye that I am?" We say with unshakable certainty, "Thou art the Christ, the Son of the living God." We say he lives! and that through him and in him we live to become again begotten sons and daughters unto God. We say this is his true and only church, that his prophets speak today, that his kingdom inexorably rolls forth to fill the whole earth with its magnificence. We say he loves all men and we must love them too. I know that my Redeemer lives and that is wonderful—wonderful to me.

3

The Inconvenient Messiah

Christ has asked demanding and difficult discipleship from the members of his church. He strengthens us for the task and he is patient with our halting efforts, but ultimately—sometime, somewhere—we have to measure up. Although that will not be easy, certainly not convenient, it will bring light to the darkest corner of our world, and it will bring life "more abundantly." In our necessary moments of self-denial, it will help to know he went that same way before.

Probably the most easily recognizable kind of evil is that which simply rebels openly against heaven, as Satan rebelled before the world was—willful, wanton opposition to God and his angels. From Cain through Caligula down to today's domestic and international hostilities, Satan has attempted to lure children of promise into violent, destructive rejection of the gospel and its teachings. These are harsh sins that the world has known only too well.

But there is another, more subtle tactic used by the primeval turncoat that is not so violent, not so vengeful, and at first glance not so vicious. But, ah, there's the rub. Because Christ and his disciples—Satan's most important and necessary targets—would never seem to be attracted by flagrant, raging wrongdoing, this second approach becomes all the more sinister. It comes in the siren's song of convenience. It is, in

26

the parlance of the day, "laid back." It says to every would-be Messiah, "Enjoy!" Its anthem might well be "Ease on Down the Road." Surely fluttering somewhere over the highway to hell is the local chamber of horrors banner reading, "Welcome to the ethics of ease."

"*Then Jesus was led up of the Spirit, into the wilderness, to be with God. And when he had fasted forty days and forty nights, and had communed with God, he was afterwards an hungered, and was left to be tempted of the devil, and when the tempter came to him, he said, If thou be the Son of God, command that these stones be made bread.*

"*But Jesus answered and said, It is written, Man shall not live by bread alone, but by every word that proceedeth out of the mouth of God.*

"*Then Jesus was taken up into the holy city, and the Spirit setteth him on the pinnacle of the temple. Then the devil came unto him and said, If thou be the Son of God, cast thyself down, for it is written, He shall give his angels charge concerning thee, and in their hands they shall bear thee up, lest at any time thou dash thy foot against a stone.*

"*And Jesus said unto him, It is written again, Thou shalt not tempt the Lord thy God.*

"*And again Jesus was in the Spirit, and it taketh him up into an exceeding high mountain, and showeth him all the kingdoms of the world and the glory of them. And the devil came unto him again, and said, All these things will I give unto thee, if thou wilt fall down and worship me.*

"*Then said Jesus unto him, Get thee hence, Satan; for it is written, Thou shalt worship the Lord thy God, and him only shalt thou serve.*

"*Then the devil leaveth him, and, behold, angels came and ministered unto him.*" (JST Matthew 4:1-10; KJV Matthew 4:11.)

One new convert to Christianity wrote of this moment: "Christ withdrew alone to the desert to fast and pray in preparation for a dialogue with the Devil. Such a dialogue was inescapable; every virtue has to be cleared with the Devil, as every vice is torn with anguish out of God's heart." (Malcolm Muggeridge, *Jesus Rediscovered,* Garden City, New York: Doubleday, 1969, p. 26.)

I believe that such dialogues are entertained day after day, hour after hour. For us, as for Christ, these temptations are far more tantalizing in their nature than the more hostile versions pursued by barbarians.

"If thou be the Son of God, command that these stones be made bread."

Whatever else Satan may do, he will certainly appeal to our appetites. Far better to play on natural, acknowledged needs than struggle to plant in us artificial ones. Here Jesus experiences the real and very understandable hunger for food by which he must sustain his mortal life. We would not deny anyone this relief; certainly we would not deny the Son of Man. Israel had its manna in the wilderness. This is Israel's God. He has fasted for forty days and forty nights. Why not eat? He seems ready to break his fast, or surely must soon. Why not simply turn the stones to bread and eat?

The temptation is *not* in the eating. He has eaten before, he will soon eat again, and he must eat for the rest of his mortal life. The temptation, at least the part I wish to focus on, is to do it *this way,* to get his bread—his physical satisfaction, relief for his human appetite—the easy way, by abuse of power and without a willingness to wait for the right time and the right way. It is the temptation to be the convenient Messiah. Why do things the hard way? Why walk to the shop—or bakery? Why travel all the way home? Why deny yourself satisfaction when with ever such a slight compromise you might enjoy this much-needed nourishment? But Christ will not ask selfishly for unearned bread. He will postpone gratification, indefinitely if necessary, rather than appease appetite—even ravenous appetite—with what is not his.

There is too much sexual transgression in our society. We

were designed and created to enjoy this highest of all physical gratifications. It is as natural as it is appealing. It is given of God to make us like God. And Satan has certainly capitalized on a divinely ordained appeal. But it is not ours without price. Not instantly. Not conveniently. Not with cozy corruption of eternal powers. It is to be earned, over time and with discipline. It, like every good thing, is God's right to bestow, not Satan's. When faced with that inherent appetite, a disciple of Christ *must* be willing to say, "<u>Yes, but *not this way.*</u>" In time, with love, after marriage. The right and proper and sanctified physical relationship of a man and a woman is as much a part— indeed, more a part—of God's plan for us as is the eating of our daily bread. But there is no convenient Messiah. <u>Salvation comes only through discipline and sacrifice.</u> Note what two historians wrote after a lifetime of studying the story of civilization:

"No one man, however brilliant or well-informed, can come in one lifetime to such fullness of understanding as to safely judge and dismiss the customs of institutions of his society, for these are the wisdom of generations after centuries of experiment in the laboratory of history. A youth boiling with hormones will wonder why he should not give full freedom to his sexual desires; and if he is unchecked by custom, morals, or laws, he may ruin his life before he matures sufficiently to understand that sex is a river of fire that must be banked and cooled by a hundred restraints if it is not to consume in chaos both the individual and the group." (Will and Ariel Durant, *The Lessons of History,* New York: Simon and Schuster, 1968, pp. 35-36.)

And we have purposes these historians never dreamed of, "promises to keep," as Robert Frost might say, "and miles to go before we sleep." I plead with us not to yield to what one has called the "glandular stench" of our times. In our hours of temptation and vulnerability I ask not to turn bread into stone with that fire that has gone unbanked and uncooled. Those loaves will be millstones—bogus bread—weighted with heartache and despair and pain. We must care more. It is too easy today with the movies we can see and the magazines we can read. It is all tragically, painfully, cunningly convenient. In our time the only restraint left is self-restraint. I ask us to say of this highest, most intimate, most sacred physical expression, "Yes, but *not this way.*" I ask us to be inconvenienced until we have earned the right and paid the divine price to know the body and the soul of the one we love.

"*If thou be the Son of God, cast thyself down from the pinnacle of this temple.*"

Satan knows this holy structure, this temple, is the center of religious life for Israel's people. It is the edifice to which the promised Messiah must come. Many are even now coming and going from their worship, many who through their traditions and disbelief will never accept Jesus as their Redeemer. Why not cast yourself down in a dramatic way and then, when the angels bear you up, as the scriptures say they must, legions will follow you and believe? They need you. You need them—to save their souls. These are covenant people. How better to help them see than to cast yourself off this holy temple unharmed and unafraid? The Messiah has indeed come.

The temptation here is even more subtle than the first. It is a temptation of the spirit, of a private hunger more real than the need for bread. Would God save him? Is Jesus to have divine companionship in this awesome ministry he now begins? He knows that among the children of men, only suffering, denunciation, betrayal, and rejection lie ahead. But what about heaven? How alone does a Messiah have to be? Perhaps before venturing forth, he ought to get final reassurance. And shouldn't Satan be silenced with his insidious "If, if, if"? Why not get spiritual confirmation, a loyal congregation, and an answer to this imp who heckles—all with one appeal to God's power? Right now. The easy way. Off the temple spire.

But Jesus refuses the temptation of the spirit. Denial and

restraint there are also part of divine preparation. He will gain followers, and he will receive reassurance. But *not this way.* Neither the converts nor the comforts he will so richly deserve have been earned yet. His ministry has hardly begun. The rewards will come by and by. But even the Son of God must wait. The Redeemer who would never bestow cheap grace on others was not likely to ask any for himself.

And so I ask us to be patient in things of the spirit. Perhaps your life has been different from mine, but I doubt it. I have had to struggle to know my standing before God. As a teenager I found it hard to pray and harder to fast. My mission was not easy. I struggled as a student only to find that I had to struggle afterwards, too. In my church and professional assignments, I have wept and ached for guidance. It seems that no worthy accomplishment has ever come easily for me, and maybe it won't for you—but I'm living long enough to be grateful for that.

It is ordained that we come to know our worth as children of God *without* something as dramatic as a leap from the pinnacle of the temple. All but a prophetic few must go about God's work in very quiet, very unspectacular ways. And as you labor to know him, and to know that he knows you; as you invest your time—and your convenience—in quiet, unassuming service, you will indeed find that "he shall give his angels charge concerning thee: and in their hands they shall bear thee up." (Matthew 4:6.) It may not come quickly. It probably won't come quickly, but there is purpose in the time it takes. We should cherish our spiritual burdens, because God will converse with us through them and will use us to do his work if we carry them well.

The spiritual odyssey of our beloved prophet, President Spencer W. Kimball, has been anything but easy. In the excerpt that follows, he describes his feelings when he was called to the apostleship. The date is July 14, 1943.

No peace had yet come, though I had prayed for it almost unceasingly. . . . I turned toward the hills. I had no objective. I wanted only to be alone. I had begun a fast. . . .

My weakness overcame me again. Hot tears came flooding down my cheeks as I made no effort to mop them up. I was accusing myself, and condemning myself and upbraiding myself. I was praying aloud for special blessings from the Lord. I was telling Him that I had not asked for this position, that I was incapable of doing the work, that I was imperfect and weak and human, that I was unworthy of so noble a calling, though I had tried hard and my heart had been right. I knew that I must have been at least partly responsible for offenses and misunderstandings which a few people fancied they had suffered at my hands. I realized that I had been petty and small many times. I did not spare myself. A thousand things passed through my mind. Was I called by revelation? . . .

If I could only have the assurance that my call had been inspired most of my other worries would be dissipated. . . . I knew that I must have His acceptance before I could go on. I stumbled up the hill and onto the mountain, as the way became rough. I faltered some as the way became steep. No paths were there to follow; I climbed on and on. Never had I prayed before as I now prayed. What I wanted and felt I must have was an assurance that I was acceptable to the Lord. I told Him that I neither wanted nor was worthy of a vision or appearance of angels or any special manifestation. I wanted only the calm peaceful assurance that my offering was accepted. Never before had I been tortured as I was now being tortured. And the assurance did not come. . . .

I mentally beat myself and chastised myself and accused myself. As the sun came up and moved in the sky I moved with it, lying in the sun, and still I received no relief. I sat up on the cliff and strange thoughts came to me: all this anguish and suffering could be ended so easily from this high cliff and then came to my mind the temptations of the Master when he was tempted to cast Himself down—then I was ashamed for having placed myself in a comparable position and trying to be dramatic. . . . I was filled with remorse because I had permitted myself to place myself . . . in a position comparable, in a small degree, to the position the Saviour found Himself in when He was tempted, and . . . I felt I had cheapened the experiences of the Lord, having compared mine with His. Again I challenged myself and told myself that I was only trying to be dramatic and sorry for myself.

. . . I lay on the cool earth. The thought came that I might take cold, but what did it matter now. There was one great desire, to get a testimony of my calling, to know that it was not human and inspired by ulterior motives, kindly as they might be. How I prayed! How I suffered! How I wept! How I struggled! (Edward L. Kimball and Andrew E. Kimball, Jr., *Spencer W. Kimball*, Salt Lake City: Bookcraft, 1977, pp. 192-95.)

More than forty years and a mountain of tumors and troubles later, this sweet and godly man continues to cling to life, *not* because that life has been convenient but because he feels there might be one more mountain to climb, one more obstacle of body or spirit that needs to be overcome.

So if your prayers don't always seem answered, take heart. One greater than you or President Kimball cried, "Eli, Eli, lama sabachthani? My God, my God, why hast thou forsaken me?" (Matthew 27:46.) If for a while the harder you try, the harder it gets, take heart. So it has been with the best people who ever lived.

Now in some frustration Satan moves right to the point. If he cannot tempt physically and cannot tempt spiritually, he will simply make an outright proposition. From a high mountain where they might overlook the kingdoms of the world and the glory of them, Satan says, "*All these things will I give thee, if thou wilt fall down and worship me.*"

Satan makes up for lack of subtlety here with the grandeur of his offer. Never mind that these kingdoms are not ultimately his to give. He simply asks of the great Jehovah, God of heaven and earth, "What is your price? Cheap bread you resist. Taw-dry messianic drama you resist, but no man can resist this world's wealth. *Name your price.*" Satan is proceeding under his first article of faithlessness—the unequivocal belief that you can buy anything in this world for money.

Jesus will one day rule the world. He will govern every principality and power in it. He will be King of kings and Lord of lords. *But not this way.* Indeed to arrive at the point at all, he has to follow a most inconvenient course. Nothing so simple as worshipping Satan or for that matter nothing so simple as wor-shipping God. At least not in the way some of us think wor-shipping is simple. His arrival at the throne of grace is to lead through travail and sorrow and sacrifice. Some seven centuries earlier Isaiah had prophesied of him, "He is despised and re-jected of men; a man of sorrows, and acquainted with grief: and we hid as it were our faces from him; he was despised, and we esteemed him not. . . . He was wounded for our transgres-sions, he was bruised for our iniquities. . . . He was oppressed, and he was afflicted, yet he opened not his mouth: he is brought as a lamb to the slaughter, and . . . openeth not his mouth." (Isaiah 53:3, 5, 7.)

Should earning our place in the kingdom of God be as difficult as that? Surely there is an easier way? Can't we buy our way in? All men and women do have a price, don't they? Sometimes we wonder. The Church has been established to extend to us the very glory of God, his intelligence, his light, and his truth. And that light and truth, by scriptural promise, is to forsake the evil one, the tempter. No, not everyone *does* have a price. Some things *can't* be purchased. Money and fame and earthly glory are not our eternal standard. Indeed these can, if we are not careful, lead to eternal torment.

Emerson said once, "Things are in the saddle, / And ride mankind." ("Ode Inscribed to W. H. Channing.") As mem-bers of the Church of Jesus Christ, we refuse to be ridden. As much as we need the wherewithal to feed and clothe ourselves and further the work of the kingdom, we do not need to sell our souls to get them. Here again, we are tempted to think there is an easy way, a fast buck, that in the world's goods and the glories of men's kingdoms, we may ride through reaping, as the very convenient Messiah. But why do we think it when it was never so for him? What do we do with a stable for birthplace and a borrowed tomb at his death? And in his lifetime? Not one single mention of earthly possessions. "The foxes have holes and the birds . . . have nests; but the Son of man hath not where to lay his head." (Matthew 8:20.)

Consider this recent news item, titled "Mormon Utah Called a Test Market for Scams":

> Utah's large Mormon population has become a prime target for con artists and swindlers who annually gyp the state's residents out of hundreds of millions of dollars. . . . Federal prosecutors say the state has gained a national reputation as "test market for scams. If it works here, they take it on the road. . . ." It has happened time and time again. . . . —It's very easy for people to bridge the gap from unbelievability to believability if church affiliation is used. . . .
>
> The investor lists were drawn up on genealogy sheets used by church members to trace their ancestry. . . . Mormon leaders denounced the scheme in a stinging editorial which asked, "Why do people take chances like this? Why do people gamble?" One answer: "Their greed gland gets stuck. . . . In this culture, financial success is often equated with righteousness." (Peter Gillins, *Sunday Star Bulletin and Advertiser*, Honolulu, January 10, 1982.)

Note also these words from Elder Marvin J. Ashton given in general conference: "In today's marketplace—yes, in your own neighborhood, town, and cities—scheming, deceiving promoters are making available to gullible purchasers all kinds of enticing offers. We are sorry to report thousands within our ranks are being duped by the glib tongues of those who offer and solicit in whispers, 'Once in a lifetime opportunities' and 'Just for you' approaches." (*Ensign*, November 1981, p. 90.) We can get our share of the earth's bounties, but *not this way*.

Speaking to this issue several years ago, Professor Hugh Nibley wrote:

> Why should we labor this unpleasant point? Because the Book of Mormon labors it, for our special benefit. Wealth is a jealous master who will not be served half-heartedly and will suffer no rival—not even God. . . . "Ye *cannot* serve God and Mammon." (Matthew 6:24.) In return for unquestioning obedience wealth promises security, power, position, and honors, in fact anything in this world. Above all, the Nephites like the Romans saw in it a mark of superiority and would do anything to get hold of it, for to them "money answereth all things." (Ecclesiastes 10:19.) . . . "Ye do always remember your riches," cried Samuel [the Lamanite], ". . . unto great swelling, envyings, strifes, malice, persecutions and murders, and all manner of iniquities." (Helaman 13:22.) Along with this, of course, everyone dresses in the height of fashion, the main point being always that the proper clothes are expensive—the expression "costly apparel" occurs 14 times in the Book of Mormon. The more important wealth is, the less important it is how one gets it. (*Since Cumorah*, Deseret Book, 1970, pp. 393-94.)

To the king who wondered if there weren't an easier way to learn, Euclid said, "Your Highness, there is no royal road to geometry"—nor any other aspect of godly knowledge. We must earn our achievements. To work hard and to try earnestly and to deserve good things to happen is worth the effort and worth the wait. And they will happen, often sooner than we think. But it won't be easy, and it won't be convenient.

May I close with a story of inconvenience. In January 1982, Air Florida's Flight 90 to Tampa, a Boeing 737 with 74 passengers aboard, began rolling down the runway at Washington's National Airport. Nothing seemed very different about this; hundreds of planes leave that airport every day. But on that day, the plane slammed into the 14th Street Bridge, smashed five cars and a truck, and then skidded into the ice-clogged river. To quote one source:

> For a moment, there was silence, and then pandemonium. Commuters watched helplessly as the plane quickly sank. . . . A few passengers bobbed to the surface; some clung numbly to pieces of debris while others screamed desperately for help. Scattered across the ice were pieces of green upholstery, twisted chunks of metal, luggage, a tennis racquet, a child's shoe. . . .
>
> Within minutes, sirens began to wail as fire trucks, ambulances and police cars rushed to the scene. A U.S. Park Police helicopter hovered overhead to pluck survivors out of the water. Six were clinging to the plane's tail. Dangling a life preserving ring to them, the chopper began ferrying them to shore. One woman had injured her right arm, so [the] pilot . . . lowered the copter until its skids touched the water; his partner [then leaned out and] scooped her up in his arms. Then [a young woman] grabbed the preserver, but as she was being helped out of the . . . river by [a] fellow passenger . . . she lost her grip. . . . A clerk for the Congressional Budget Office who was watching from the shore plunged into the water and dragged her to land. But the most notable act of heroism was performed by [another] of the passengers, a balding man in his early 50s. Each time the ring was lowered, he grabbed it and passed it along to a comrade; when the helicopter finally returned to pick him up, he had disappeared beneath the ice. (James Kelly, "We're Not Going to Make It," *Time*, January 25, 1982, pp. 16-17.)

I quote now from an essay entitled simply "The Man in the Water":

> His selflessness [is] one reason the story held national attention; his anonymity another. The fact that he [has gone] unidentified invests him with a universal character. For a

37

while he was Everyman, and thus proof (as if one needed it) that no man is ordinary.

Still, he could never have imagined such a capacity in himself. Only minutes before his character was tested, he was sitting in the ordinary plane among the ordinary passengers, dutifully listening to the stewardess telling him to fasten his seat belt and saying something about the "no smoking sign." So our man relaxed with the others, some of whom would owe their lives to him. Perhaps he started to read, or to doze, or to regret some harsh remark made in the office that morning. Then suddenly he knew that the trip would not be ordinary. Like every other person on that flight, he was desperate to live, which makes his final act so stunning.

For at some moment in the water he must have realized that he would not live if he continued to hand over the rope and ring to others. He *had* to know it, no matter how gradual the effect of the cold. In his judgment he had no choice. When the helicopter took off with what was to be the last survivor, he watched everything in [his] world move away from him, and he deliberately let it [go]. . . .

The odd thing is that we do not . . . really believe that the man in the water lost his fight. . . . He could not, [like Nature], make ice storms, or freeze the water until it froze the blood. But he could hand life over to a stranger, and that is a power of nature too. The man in the water pitted himself against an implacable, impersonal enemy; he fought it with charity; and he [won]. (Roger Rosenblatt, *Time*, January 25, 1982, p. 86. Copyright 1982 Time Inc. All rights reserved. Reprinted by permission from TIME.)

In this world we are all, you and I, the man or the woman in the water. We often must, like this man and Hamlet, "take arms against a sea of troubles, and by opposing end them." (Act 3, scene 1, 11. 59-60.) And sometimes the cost is very high. It was for Christ, it was for Joseph Smith, and it was for this lone man who counted the cost there in the Potomac—

and paid it. It is not easy to go without—without physical gratifications or spiritual assurances or material possessions, but sometimes we must, since there is no guarantee of convenience written into our Christian covenant. We must work hard and do right, as Abraham Lincoln said, and sometime our chance will come. And when we've tried, really tried, and waited for what seemed never to be ours, *then* we may experience what the Savior experienced when "the angels came, and ministered unto him." (Matthew 4:11.) Surely that is worth waiting for.

4

The Meaning of Membership: A Personal Response

It is important to remember that God often answers our prayers through the expressions and actions of other people. By the same token, we ought to live in such a way that he can use us to answer prayers for them. In times of need, no people should be "strangers and foreigners, but [rather] fellowcitizens with the saints." Such association and proximity are part of the divine purpose of The Church of Jesus Christ of Latter-day Saints.

I am not much of a joiner. I didn't belong to many clubs or social units at school, and more recently I have been about as reluctant in my professional affiliations. Some of my assignments have required public participation, but in many other ways I am a private person. My sentiments are not quite those of Robert Frost, but they are close. To a group of young people he once said: "Don't join too many gangs. Join your family and join the United States and drop off at a college on the way if you have time, but don't join a lot of gangs."

In addition to joining my family and the United States and dropping by a college because I had time, I have made one other commitment more important than all the rest. Indeed, it is the commitment that gives meaning to all of my other associations, personal or professional, public or private. I am a

member of The Church of Jesus Christ of Latter-day Saints—
baptized, confirmed, ordained, endowed. A veritable pacifist
when it comes to social guilds or luncheon clubs, I turn into
something of a militant on the subject of the only true and living church on the face of the earth. As an ancient prophet declared, I have wanted above any other fraternal relationship to
"come into the fold of God, and to be called his people."
(Mosiah 18:8.)

What does it mean to belong, to be a member of Christ's
church and be "called unto the fellowship of . . . Jesus Christ
our Lord"? (1 Corinthians 1:9.) Obviously much of the joy and
most of the meaning is yet to be fully realized. Surely it will be
after death and beyond the veil that, more mature and enlightened, we will see—because we will be shown—the eternal
implications of our earthly covenants. But what of our experience now? What does membership mean to us today, while we
yet live and exert our faith and confront our problems in this
world? What do we find while we wait, looking toward a celestial reward that does not come in mortality?

Let me share a personal response to those questions with
two caveats: First, no single statement can do justice to what
any of us feel about our church membership; a barrel of books
could not do it, and certainly the little cup I am offering will
not contain it. Second, the most personal of responses—and
consequently the most persuasive ones—cannot be shared.
Some are too sacred and others simply ineffable. In either case,
all that can be put in the briefest of print is, as Ammon said,
"the smallest part" of what we feel. (Alma 26:16.)

Obviously part of the meaning of being a "member" is in
that choice of language itself, coined originally by the apostle
Paul who knew so much about coming to Christ: "As the body
is one, and hath many members, . . . so also is Christ. . . .
For the body is not one member but many. . . . And the eye
cannot say unto the hand, I have no need of thee: nor again

the head to the feet, I have no need of you. . . . Now ye are the body of Christ, and members in particular." (1 Corinthians 12:12, 14, 21, 27.)

It is an immensely satisfying thing to be needed in the body of Christ. Whether I function as an eye or an arm is irrelevant; the fact is, I am needed in this most majestic organism, and the body is imperfect without me. A popular singer made a small fortune reminding us that "people who need people are the luckiest people in the world." In The Church of Jesus Christ of Latter-day Saints, the restored ecclesiastical body of Christ, people do need people and everyone is welcomed. This includes (in Paul's assertion) not only the attractive, talented, "comely" members, but also those of us who seem to have fewer gifts and face greater challenges, those who receive less honor and attention. In the Church of Jesus Christ "more abundant honor" is given to these. Every member matters, and the less favored member most of all. (See 1 Corinthians 12:23-24.)

For most of the first two decades of my life I attended one ward of the Church—the old St. George Fifth Ward. Now, after two more decades, it is a moving memory for me to sit all alone in that darkened red sandstone tabernacle so artistically crafted by loving pioneer hands. That is the meetinghouse of the "members" where I was confirmed into the "body of Christ." That is where I went to Primary and first passed the sacrament as a nervous and uncertain deacon. That is the pulpit where I gave my first talk and the podium where I shook the hand of President George Albert Smith the year I was baptized. It was there that I sat spellbound in that ornate balcony as Elder Matthew Cowley brought the audience to both laughter and tears on a visit to our stake conference. I was hardly an eye or an ear then; more like a lash or a lobe, I suppose. But I was an irreplaceable member of the body of Christ.

Since then I have lived and loved and been loved in a dozen other wards of the Church, and the blessings of church assignments have taken me to many dozen more. But always and everywhere it is the same, whether in an open-air, hand-hewn South Pacific *fale* or the striking Hyde Park Chapel on Exhibition Road in London. Wherever I have attended church at home or abroad, it has evoked the same meaning of that beautiful old tabernacle where I was first part of the congregation. Latter-day Saints love and welcome and reach out in a way that Christians are commanded to do. Indeed, there are "no more strangers and foreigners" in the household of God. (Ephesians 2:19.) We have been commanded to "meet together oft, to fast and to pray, and to speak one with another concerning the welfare of [our] souls." (Moroni 6:5.) This is something more than boys clubs or civic associations or political affiliations offer, worthy as those may be. It is more than house parties and welcome wagons provide, as kind as such expressions are. This fellowship is ultimately of the spirit, and it comes because Christ is our eternal head.

In the aftermath of the Teton Dam disaster that swept floodwaters through the Upper Snake River Valley in southeastern Idaho, many of our friends there reported very inspiring personal experiences. Combined, they read something like this:

"We didn't cry when we saw our home ripped away from its foundation. We didn't cry when we thought of the photo albums and ordination certificates and irreplaceable personal treasures that would be gone forever. We didn't cry as we fought for everything we could save and repeatedly counted heads through the neighborhood to make sure lives were safe.

"But later on, when we looked up and saw out of the night those buses and vans and jeeps and pickups rumbling toward us like an armored division of a heavenly army, we sat down and sobbed. Old people and young people and artisans and laborers, 45,000 of them. They came from everywhere for hundreds of miles—over some roads still uncleared and unsafe. They tumbled out of those buses with shovels and buckets and hammers and food. 'It looks like you could use a hand,' they would say, laughing to keep back the tears at what they saw before them. Then shoulder to shoulder with friends we had never seen before and may never see again, we cleaned and sang and held each other up.

"We cried then and then only—not about the flood, but about what happened after it. We can't discuss it now without the memory of a hymn ringing in our ears:

> When through the deep waters I call thee to go,
> The rivers of sorrow shall not thee o'erflow,
> For I will be with thee thy troubles to bless,
> And sanctify to thee thy deepest distress.
>
> The soul that on Jesus hath leaned for repose
> I will not, I cannot, desert to his foes,
> That soul, though all hell should endeavor to shake
> I'll never, no never, no never forsake.
> —*Hymns*, no. 66

It *is* a soul-stirring reassurance to belong, to be part of the most cohesive extended-family association in all eternity. We speak of sealing ourselves to one another, and well we should. The Prophet Joseph Smith said we might more plainly refer to it as welding. (D&C 128:18.) The bonding and brotherhood are unmistaken. Setting aside for a time the heavenly host we hope one day to enjoy, I still choose the Church of Jesus Christ to fill my need to be needed—here and now, as well as there and then. When public problems or private heartaches come—as surely they do come—I will be most fortunate if in that hour I find myself in the company of Latter-day Saints.

What emerges from that special association—from feelings of safety and peace, of belonging and happiness and heavenly help—is an inexorable sense of purpose and direction. Some have felt the fears and frustrations of life more than others, but all of us feel them a little, and in such times we need the gospel compass to remind us who we are and where we must go.

Blaise Pascal, probably France's most notable child prodigy of the last three centuries, reflects in an extreme way what many men have felt when unaided by gospel truths. He wrote of his very gifted life, "When I see the blindness and wretchedness of man, when I regard the whole silent universe and man without light, left to himself, and, as it were, lost in this corner of the universe, without knowing who has put him there, what he has come to do, what will become of him at death, and incapable of all knowledge, I become terrified, like a man who should be carried in his sleep to a dreadful desert island and should awake without knowing where he is and without means of escape." (*Pensées,* XI, 693.)

Contrast that psychic turbulence with the serenity we saw while standing with our childhood playmates as they laid their first-born child in the grave. This beautiful little thirteen-year-old girl, born just ninety days after our own first child, had fallen victim to Cockayne's syndrome a half dozen years earlier. There is no way to adequately describe the deterioration of that little body now gone. Nor is there any way to tell the patience and the pain of those parents as they carried legs that could not walk and finally fed with an eye-dropper a mouth that could not swallow.

But there was no existential anguish rending the air. Standing quietly—no, peacefully—at the casket with this little family now temporarily lessened by Patti's leaving were her Beehive class, her Sunday School teacher, and a favorite teenage home teacher. There also were the two with whom her father had served in the bishopric. Her mother's Relief Society associates dried their tears and slipped away to prepare a family luncheon. Fellow members in the body of Christ remembered, "And whether one member suffer, all the members suffer with it." (1 Corinthians 12:26.)

In that circle, these were the graveside lyrics of a loving neighbor, lines sung in this setting not for their sentiment but for their theology:

Do you know who you are, little child of mine,
So precious and dear to me?
Do you know you are a part of a great design
That is vast as eternity? . . .
Do you know you're a child of God?

Do you know where you're going, child of mine?
Are your eyes on the road ahead?
Do the spires of his castle gleam and shine
Where the sun grows golden red? . . .
You will make it, my child, I know.
　　　　　—Ora Pate Stewart, "To a Child"

That hopeful, trusting facing of the future is part of what it means to be a Latter-day Saint. It is part of knowing by divine revelation the answers (even in our childhood) to life's greatest questions. One writer speaking for almost all others declared that "the whole interest of [philosophy] . . . is centered in the three following questions: 1. What can I know? 2. What ought I to do? 3. What may I hope?" (Immanuel Kant, *Critique of Pure Reason.*) Think of those fundamental and ancient issues, think of Pascalean terror, and then stand again at that little child's grave.

We have no way to measure such a conviction, but I am confident that tiny girl knew more of the eternal meaning of her experience than most of the adult population on this planet would have known in similar circumstances. And why not? Why shouldn't it intensify our sense of identity and self-respect and hope for the future to know that we are the spiritual offspring of God, that he is literally our Father in heaven, and that we are by lineal descent his sons and daughters, created in his own image? What encouragement should it give us to know that we lived with him before memory was revoked and that we will be with him again when all things, including memory, are fully restored? That one abiding

46

and ineluctable truth does more to answer the philosophical questions of six millennia than any other single assertion under heaven. Indeed, man is only slightly under heaven, "a little lower than the angels" (Psalm 8:5), and never out of divine reach.

In the midst of a brutal Civil War, Abraham Lincoln fought off depression and asked the nation to fight it too. "It is difficult to make a man miserable," he said, "while [that man] feels worthy of himself and claims kindred to the great God who made him." (Speech delivered September 14, 1862.) When times are difficult or the unknown confronts us, it is impossible to measure the peaceful reassurance of those undeniable promises given to us from "cloven tongues like as of fire." (Acts 2:3.)

The Savior asked, "What man is there of you, whom if his son asks bread, will he give him a stone? Or if he ask a fish, will he give him a serpent? If ye then, being evil, know how to give good gifts unto your children, how much more shall your Father which is in heaven give good things to them that ask him?" (Matthew 7:9-11.) To my beloved Pat and me, our children are more precious possessions than any crown or kingdom this world could offer. There is literally not anything in righteousness we would not do for them; there is no stream so deep nor mountain so high nor desert so wide that we could be kept from calming their fears or holding them close to us. And if we "being evil" can love so much and try so hard, what *does* that say of a more Godly love that differs from our own as the stars differ from the sun? On a particularly difficult day, or sometimes a series of difficult days, what would this world's inhabitants pay to know that heavenly parents are reaching across those same streams and mountains and deserts, anxious to hold them close? That manifest reassurance comes in its fullest form only in the doctrines and the covenants of The Church of Jesus Christ of Latter-day Saints. What a soothing strength that gives in a world—even a religious world—spoken of by C. S. Lewis as being full of otherwise "cold Christs and tangled trinities."

President Harold B. Lee, in the keynote address of the last general conference he ever faced, said that this understanding of who we are is "of first importance," and without it we lack the basis "of a solid foundation upon which to build our lives." (*Conference Report*, October 1973, p. 5.) That solid foundation is the same that the Savior himself declared to be crucial in the day when rains descend and floods come and winds blow. Part of that gospel strength is simply and magnificently the knowledge of who we are. However, so much that we find in our daily experience is in opposition to that knowledge and would blind us to our strength. One man wrote that to be what we really are "in a world which is doing its best, night and day, to make you something else means to fight the hardest battle which any human being can fight." (E. E. Cummings.) What we "really are" is embryonic gods, and surely this world is trying to make us forget that, make us pursue something else. It does not take a theologian to recognize that *anything* else will be a tragic disappointment in the strictest prophetic as well as Aristotelian sense.

We must remember, in a world where some still go hungry, that men, women, and children can starve from a lack of self-knowledge as much as they can from a lack of bread. That is why, when Jesus invited his disciples to partake of the emblems of his body and blood, they were filled (3 Nephi 18:4-5)—filled with the spirit of heaven, filled with the spirit of hope, filled with more certain knowledge of who they really were: "heirs of God, and joint heirs with Christ." That same spirit bears witness to us yet that we are the children of God. (Romans 8:16-17.) Indeed, as President Lee (and every other prophetic voice) has declared, "the first thing to be done to help a man to moral regeneration is to restore, if possible, his self-respect."

(Lee, *op. cit.*) The gospel of Jesus Christ does that for its members in a unique and inimitable way.

When asked "What can I know?", a Latter-day Saint answers, "All that God knows." When asked "What ought I to do?", his disciples answer, "Follow the Master." When asked "What may I hope?", an entire dispensation declares, "Peace in this world and eternal life in the world to come" (D&C 59:23), indeed ultimately for "all that [the] Father hath" (D&C 84:38). Depressions and identity crises have a hard time holding up under that.

Latter-day Saints also enjoy the privilege of special reminders to these truths. Every baptized and confirmed member of The Church of Jesus Christ of Latter-day Saints has received the sacred gift of the Holy Ghost. Its unlimited power to teach, guide, comfort, and witness is not fully known or available outside the true church. No personal counsel from any other source compares with it in degree of constancy or conviction. It will show us "all things" that we should do. (2 Nephi 32:5.) Perhaps that is why, when asked by the president of the United States how The Church of Jesus Christ of Latter-day Saints differed from other religions of the day, the Prophet Joseph Smith noted baptism and the gift of the Holy Ghost, believing that "all other considerations were contained in the Gift of the Holy Ghost." (*History of the Church* 4:42.) The Holy Ghost is a revelator, and no other sin is so great as the sin against its promise.

In addition, we are blessed with both ancient and modern scripture. All men and women have access to the Old and New Testaments, but to them the restored gospel adds hundreds and hundreds of pages of additional revealed testimony. Furthermore, there are the uncanonized but equally prophetic statements of twelve (equaling the entire number of so-called "minor prophets" in the Old Testament!) successive, living prophets covering over 150 years of our own dispensation.

We cannot but wonder what frenzy the world would experience if a chapter of the Book of Mormon or a section of the Doctrine and Covenants (or a conference address by President Spencer W. Kimball) were to be discovered by some playful shepherd boy in an earthen jar near the Dead Sea caves of Qumran. The beneficiaries would probably build a special shrine in Jerusalem to house it, being very careful to regulate temperatures and restrict visitors. They would undoubtedly protect it against earthquakes and war. Surely the edifice would be as beautiful as the contents would be valuable; its cost would be enormous, but its worth would be incalculable. Yet for the most part we have difficulty *giving away* copies of sacred scripture much more startling in their origin. Worse yet, some of us, knowing of the scriptures, have not even tried to share them, as if an angel were an everyday visitor and a prophet just another man in the street. We forget that our fathers lived for many centuries without priesthood power or prophetic leadership, and "dark ages" they were indeed.

Occasionally in our own time we are given a sharp reminder of how precious our privilege is. As a church we have often wanted to pray in a special way for the health of President Kimball. Anyone who has felt his touch or lingered in his embrace knows why we care so much. During one of President Kimball's hospitalizations, our children decided with us to fast for him. I wept with pride as I watched those children endure silently and bravely this unexpected sacrifice. Even our youngest at five saw it through and made his widow's mite count toward the health of the prophet. Our oldest at thirteen said it all in his own manly way: "The younger children probably couldn't do it, Dad, if it were for anyone else but President Kimball." We feel about having a prophet's leadership as someone felt of the rising sun—that if it came but once a year instead of every day, oh, what would be the anticipation! We thank thee, O God, for a prophet.

There are a thousand reasons for and ten thousand joys in

belonging to the true church. Surely no one can fully say—perhaps not even begin to say—what that covenantal relationship means to him or her. Suffice it to say that those who believe with me that The Church of Jesus Christ of Latter-day Saints is indeed the restoration of pure Christianity in the fullness of time will understand the meaning of membership expressed by an early seeker of the truth who fell during the Roman persecutions of the third century. Before he died, Cyprian wrote to his friend Donatus: "This seems a cheerful world, Donatus, when I view it from this fair garden under the shadow of these vines. But if I climbed some great mountain and looked over the wide lands, you know very well what I would see—brigands on the high roads, pirates on the seas, in the amphitheaters men murdered to please applauding crowds; under all roofs misery and selfishness. It is really a bad world, yet in the midst of it I have found a quiet and holy people. They have discovered a joy which is a thousand times better than any pleasure of this sinful life. They are despised and persecuted, but they care not. They have overcome the world. These people, Donatus, are the Christians and I am one of them." (Quoted by Marion D. Hanks, "Freedom and Responsibility," BYU *Speeches of the Year*, May 28, 1964, p. 11.)

Following a long night of darkness, "these people" are the Latter-day Saints—and I am one of them. The meaning of my life is inextricably linked with my membership in that body. There my family and friends have found life, and found it "more abundantly."

5

Borne upon Eagles' Wings

All of us feel limitations of one kind or another. These might be emotional or social or physical or cultural, but we all have feelings of inadequacy and we all feel we have made some mistakes. A visitor's experience inside a prison gives a rare view of the result of such extreme mistakes, while providing a poignant reminder of other kinds of bondage we inflict on ourselves. We ought to learn from these penalties that are imposed and rise above them to true freedom.

It was unlike any other commencement or baccalaureate exercise I had ever attended. There were forty-four graduates, all male. They did not have traditional academic robes or caps or gowns. Their attire, to a man, was light blue denim shirts and dark blue denim trousers. The ceremony was not held in a fieldhouse or a stadium or even a lovely auditorium. The exercise was held in a modest interdenominational chapel at the Utah state prison. The graduating class consisted of forty-four men who had successfully completed a year's course of Bible study sponsored by The Church of Jesus Christ of Latter-day Saints but open to all who cared to come and participate. These forty-four represented more than a dozen different religions, and, of course, many of them had no formal religious affiliation at all.

A delightfully cordial and capable inmate conducted the

exercises. He immediately warmed the group to the event. About half were pleasantly and appropriately called "outsiders." He said he wanted the outsiders particularly to appreciate that he was in prison even though he had hired one of the biggest criminal lawyers in America: "It was only after I was through with the trial that I fully understood that designation," he said. "He thought he was a lawyer and I think he's a criminal."

The opening prayer was given by a young man who seemed like a boy and looked like a boy and surely had not yet begun to shave. He gave there, according to the chaplain, the first verbal and public prayer he had ever given in his life. He was frightened to death, but it was a prayer of the heart, and you would need to have been there and to have heard it to appreciate it fully. He was in the prison for ten years to life on an armed robbery charge. The closing prayer was given by a man who was, I suppose, forty-five or fifty years old—a pleasant, slightly chubby man who looked as if he should have been somebody's uncle and undoubtedly was. He was in for a life term on second-degree murder.

The choir sang, among other numbers, the Hammerstein-Romberg song "Stouthearted Men." The looks on their faces and the feeling in their voices said something about stouthearted men that I had never understood before. I don't think any two of them crossed paths on the same note at any given moment during the rendition. But it was a choir of angels. When they sang, "Give me some men who are stouthearted men, who will fight for the rights they adore; / Give me ten men who are stouthearted men, and I'll soon give you ten thousand more," they knew something about rights that had been adored and lost, that were adored all the more because they had been lost, and that perhaps were desired more greatly because someday they might return.

A young man who was now on the outside had come back to get his certificate and to encourage his colleagues. He said something that I wrote down. He looked out to his colleagues and said, "Guys, the perspective in prison is really bad. Things really look better on the outside. Try to remember that." Then he turned to the outsiders, to the friends and families who had come in, and said, "You people are a light in a dark place. If it were not for love like yours, we would not be able to get from where we are to where we need to be."

He was followed by another delightful young man who couldn't have been more than twenty years of age. He had been in and out of prison very quickly—only eight months and then probation. He talked about what it was like to be back out, to be holding a job, dating girls, going to church, and trying to live a moral and law-abiding life. He turned to friend and stranger alike and said, "Please understand that those of us at the halfway house need faith and prayers too. We have reentered a world of temptation."

The inmate who conducted the service concluded with some emotion in his voice and tears in his eyes. "This is the most auspicious occasion of our year," he said of this graduation service. "It is better than Christmas. It's better than Thanksgiving. It's even better than Mother's Day. It's better because we're enlightened, and that's as close as we come to being free."

Then the gates clanged behind my wife and me and we went home. But I have never forgotten the experience and the impressions I had that evening. One thought I had profoundly impressed upon me is that God is just. Alma said, "What, do ye suppose that mercy can rob justice? I say unto you, Nay; not one whit. If so, God would cease to be God." (Alma 42:25.) Paul said to the Galatians, "Be not deceived; God is not mocked: for whatsoever a man soweth, that shall he also reap." (Galatians 6:7.) If we sow thistles, we shouldn't plan to get strawberries. If we sow hate, we must not expect to reap an abundance of love. We get back, in kind, that which we reap, but we reap, somehow, always in greater quantity. We sow a little thistle, and we get a lot of thistle—years and years of it, big bushes and branches of it. We never get rid of it unless we cut it out. If we sow a little bit of hate, before we know it we've reaped a lot of hate—smoldering and festering and belligerent and finally warring and malicious hate.

A prophet of the Old Testament, Hosea, warned all of us to be careful lest we learn personally something that I think my friends at the state institution understood more fully than I had: "They have sown the wind, and they shall reap the whirlwind." (Hosea 8:7.) God is just. We really do reap what we sow.

Then I had the comforting idea that my first thought wasn't as painful as it sounded. However frightening it may be to realize that all of us have sinned, however frightening it may be to contemplate a just God, surely it is infinitely more frightening to contemplate an unjust God.

A basic principle of Latter-day Saint doctrine is that in order to go forward, we have to know that God is just. Joseph Smith's *Lectures on Faith* give a basic list of attributes God must have (which we know he does have) in order for us to have faith in him, principles that give us the courage to believe that it will be well with us if we obey his commandments. One of those Godly attributes is justice. We would not have the faith to live righteously or to love better or to repent more readily if we did not think that justice would count for us, if we thought that God would change his mind midstream and tell us there was another set of rules in force. Because we know that God is just and would cease to be God if he were unjust, we have the faith to go forward knowing we will not be the victims of whimsy or caprice or a bad day or a bad joke.

A third thought came to me. How grateful I was that, in addition to being just, God is able to be merciful also. After Alma had established with Corianton that God has to be just, he then stressed that that same God would be merciful as well, and that mercy would claim the *penitent*. (See Alma 42.) That concept meant a bit more to me because I had just been where they added *i-a-r-y* to that word. Alma gave me encouragement: mercy could claim the penitent. I decided that if those men had to go to the penitentiary to take advantage of the gift of mercy, if somehow by going there they were repenting and finding the gospel of Jesus Christ or the scriptures or the power of the Atonement, then their imprisonment was worth it. We should all go to the penitentiary, or to the bishop, or to the Lord, or to those whom we have offended or to those who have offended us. Our own little penitentiaries are all around us. If acknowledgment of that is what it takes to make us truly penitent, to enable us to lay claim to the gift of mercy, then we must "serve our time."

I know it isn't easy to go back and to undo and to make a new beginning, but I believe with all my heart that it is easier to begin anew than it is to go on believing that justice will not take its toll. As Elder Richard L. Evans was fond of saying, "What's the use of running if you're on the wrong road?" A favorite British scholar said, using the same metaphor, "I do not think that all who choose wrong roads perish; but their rescue consists in being put back on the right road. A [mathematical] sum [incorrectly worked] can be put right; but only by going back till you find the error and then working it fresh from that point. [It will] never [be corrected] by simply *going on.* Evil can be undone, but it cannot 'develop' into good. Time does not heal it. The spell must be unwound." (C. S. Lewis, *The Great Divorce,* New York: Macmillan Co., 1973, p. 6.) God is just, but mercy claimeth the penitent, and the evil can be undone. There is some repenting to be done in every life, and we ought to be about it.

One thing we ought to repent of is our own ignorance. There are little clichés we learn early in our lives, most of which I dislike; some of them I *really* dislike. I think number one on my list is "Sticks and stones will break my bones, but names will never hurt me." Names do hurt. I'll take sticks and stones any day. Second to this are the clichés "Ignorance is bliss" and "What I don't know won't hurt me." Those two are really dangerous. In fact, I believe that nothing will hurt us more than what we don't know.

Plato said, "It is better to be unborn than untaught, for ignorance is at the root of all misfortune." Samuel Johnson said, "Ignorance, *when voluntary*, is criminal, and a man may be properly charged with that evil which he neglected or refused to learn how to prevent." (Italics added.) But I don't want to talk just about Plato's books and Sam Johnson's books. We *ought* to read those works, but we *must* read the word of God. At one time in the history of the Church in this dispensation, the entire church was indicted for not doing so. In 1832, in a revelation given through the Prophet Joseph Smith, the Lord declared:

"I now give unto you a commandment to beware concerning yourselves, to give diligent heed to the *words* of eternal life. For you shall live by every *word* that proceedeth forth from the mouth of God. For the *word* of the Lord is truth, and whatsoever is truth is light, and whatsoever is light is Spirit, even the Spirit of Jesus Christ." (D&C 84:43-45. Italics added.)

The first rung of this ladder that brings us the Spirit of Christ is the *word,* and to disregard the word—especially the Book of Mormon—is to cut off that light which is Spirit. "Your minds in times past have been darkened because of unbelief, and because you have treated lightly the things you have received . . . even the Book of Mormon and the former commandments which I have given." (D&C 84:54, 57.)

Can we, like these early Saints, also be accused of taking this book lightly? Some of us treat it as if it were just another book—let it gather a little dust, or use it to press the rose from Mary Jane's wedding, or use it as a doorstop in the hallway, or do almost anything with it but read it. I believe we will be indicted for the darkness we incur and that we will owe penitence in this life or the next for that which we fail to learn, especially that which we fail to learn from the Book of Mormon. President Joseph Fielding Smith taught that "no member of this church can stand approved in the presence of God who has not seriously and carefully read the Book of Mormon." (*Conference Report,* October 1961, p. 18.)

Too often we are also in servitude to our own bodies. Paul said, "I delight in the law of God after the inward man: but I see another law in my members, warring against the law of my mind, and bringing me into captivity." (Romans 7:22-23.) I don't mean just the dramatic sins—the anger that leads to murder, or the passion that leads to sexual transgression, or the lust that leads to theft. There are more common kinds of bondage than these. The war in the body of someone who is a little overweight that makes him huff and puff by the time he gets to the top of the stairs, the war of the mattress on his back that he somehow cannot shake in the morning so he misses those precious and most inspirational hours of the day, the war of grooming and personal hygiene that could do much for us—all these are restrictive to our freedom if we don't control them. But of course certain limitations are sometimes beyond our control.

Some time ago I met a man I would like to meet again. His name is Henry D. Stagg—Don Stagg to his friends. He went to bed in August of 1965 about the way everybody else goes to bed and about the way he had all of his life. The difference came the next morning when his body awoke and his eyes didn't. He was blind and he was frightened. He went to his doctor, who said, with guarded optimism, "This thing sometimes doesn't last very long, and it might just be an hour or two." Well, the hours stretched into days and the days stretched into weeks and the weeks finally became a month. Don Stagg could think of only one thing, and that was suicide.

To make a long story short, Don Stagg found, in the midst of his experience, what one of the prisoners found; that is, it takes some love to get from where we are to where we need to be. One evening Mrs. Stagg arranged to slip the children past the hospital security. They shuffled into the room, but of course Don did not know who was there. By his own admission, he was surly and despondent almost all of the time, and he didn't want to talk. But then he felt those little hands on his legs and on his arms. The children said, "Daddy, we love you, and we want you to come home. We don't want any other daddy."

Figuratively but not literally, Don had seen a little light in a dark place, so he went home and started to pace off distances in the house. He first paced off the steps from the bedroom to the refrigerator, thinking, "It's one thing to be blind; it's another thing to starve to death." When he had the house mastered, he went out into the neighborhood and then up and down the streets for several miles. He decided that he could do a lot more than he thought he could. About two years after the effects of this disease had taken his sight, he enrolled in law school at the University of Utah. In four years he passed all his courses and the state bar. For one year he worked for the attorney general's office, and now he is in private practice.

Don Stagg is blind and has some limitations and some bonds put upon him by his own body, but he is doing a great deal. He water-skis and he snow-skis and he can play a great game of golf. Now, there are some things he can't do. He cannot see the daughter who has been born to him since he lost his sight. But he believes he will someday.

Life itself—our various cultural and environmental circumstances—can also impose some severe bonds upon us. We may be perfectly healthy, have fine bodies, and even know a good deal about the gospel, but life still may have cast us in roles that we cannot seem to escape. In discussing limitations of birth and circumstances, I remember the very famous story that Elder Marion D. Hanks told me as a missionary:

The famed naturalist of the last century, Louis Agassiz, was lecturing in London and had done a marvelous job. An obviously bright little old lady, but one who did not seem to have all the advantages in life, came up and was spiteful. She was resentful and said that she had never had the chances that he had had and she hoped he appreciated it. He took that bit of a lacing very pleasantly and turned to the lady and, when she was through, said, "What do you do?"

She said, "I run a boarding house with my sister. I'm unmarried."

"What do you do at the boarding house?"

"Well, I skin potatoes and chop onions for the stew. We have stew every day."

"Where do you sit when you do that interesting but homely task?"

"I sit on the bottom step of the kitchen stairs."

"Where do your feet rest when you sit there on the bottom step?"

"On a glazed brick."

"What's a glazed brick?"

"I don't know."

"How long have you been sitting there?"

"Fifteen years."

Agassiz concluded, "Here's my card. Would you write me a note when you get a moment about what a glazed brick is?"

Well, that made her mad enough to go home and do it. She went home and got the dictionary out and found out that a brick was a piece of baked clay. That didn't seem enough to send to a Harvard professor, so she went to the encyclopedia and found out that a brick was made of vitrified kaolin and hydrous aluminum silicate, which didn't mean a thing to her. She went to work and visited a brick factory and a tile maker. Then she went back in history and studied a little bit about geology and learned something about clay and clay beds and what *hydrous* meant and what *vitrified* meant. She began to soar out of the basement of a boarding house on the wings of words like *vitrified kaolin* and *hydrous aluminum silicate*. She finally decided that there were about 120 different kinds of glazed bricks and tiles. She could tell Agassiz that, so she wrote him a little note of thirty-six pages and said, "Here's your glazed brick."

He wrote back, "This is a fine piece of work. If you change this and that and the other, I'll prepare it for publication and send you that which is due you from the publication." She thought no more of it, made the changes, sent it back, and almost by return mail came a check for 250 dollars. His letter said, "I've published your piece. What was under the brick?"

And she said, "Ants."

He replied (all of this by mail), "What's an ant?"

She went to work and this time she was excited. She found 1825 different kinds of ants. She found that there were ants that you could put three to the head of a pin and still have standing room left over. She found that there were ants an inch long that moved in armies half a mile wide and destroyed everything in their path. She found that some ants were blind; some ants lost their wings on the afternoon they died; some milked cows and took the milk to the aristocrats up the street. She found more ants than anybody had ever found, so she wrote Mr. Agassiz something of a treatise, numbering 360 pages. He published it and sent her the money and royalties, which continued to come in. She saw the lands and places of her dreams on a little carpet of vitrified kaolin and on the wings of flying ants that may lose their wings on the afternoon they die. (*The Gift of Self*, Salt Lake City: Bookcraft, 1974, pp. 151-53.)

I do not minimize the limitations of our circumstance and our environment and the battle we have in order to overcome them. I know there can be real fetters, but perhaps we can do something about them. For all I know, we may all be sitting with our feet on glazed bricks.

Let me just conclude this thought about various kinds of bondage with one more example. We may be bright and learned. We may be physically fit and fully capable. We may have all of the advantages of circumstance and environment and society. But there is a bondage and a servitude and a limitation that, if we're not careful, may be more subtle and seductive than any of the others. For lack of something else to call it, let me call it the world. May I share with you a few lines on this subject:

> For that person striving to live righteously, this mortal existence is a testing time indeed. The faithful are plagued with the temptations of a world that appears to have lost itself in a snarled maze of ambiguity, mendacity, and threatening uncertainty. The challenge to live in the world but not of the world is a monumental one, indeed.
>
> Our second estate is indeed a probationary state. The choices we are called upon to make every day of our lives call forth the exercise of our agency. That we fail so frequently to think and do that which is right is not evidence against the practicality of righteous living. We do not falter and stumble in the path of righteousness simply because we do nothing else, but because too often we lose the vision of our relationship with God. The incessant din and cackling ado of this turbulent life drown out the message which asserts that, as man is, God once was, and that as God is, man may become.
>
> If we will not dance to the music of materialism and hedonism but will remain attuned to the voice of godly reason, we will be led to the green pastures of respite and the still waters of spiritual refreshment. All the slings and arrows of outrageous fortune this world can hurl against us are as nothing when compared to the rewards for steadfastness and faithfulness. It would behoove us all to fix our sights more consistently upon the things which are everlasting and eternal. This world is not our home.

Those lines are from the valedictory address at the Utah state prison graduation exercise I mentioned at the outset. The speaker was about fifty years of age and has been behind bars for more than half of those years. He knows whereof he speaks.

If we had to explain to someone the reasons for our mortal existence, that explanation would have to include something about freedom. An important part of the great council in heaven dealt with freedom and how it would be exercised. The Father's course was one of agency and choice and freedom to err, but ultimately freedom to succeed. As many safeguards as possible, including the revelatory powers of heaven, were brought to enlighten our choices so that freedom would not turn to bondage.

What a fortunate time we live in, because our prophet is not incarcerated. If you took the sum total of religious history in the dispensations down to and including our own, you would probably find the saints in prison much of the time: Israel in servitude or escaping from some Egyptians, Nephites escaping from Lamanites, the Prophet Joseph in Liberty jail, or the rest of us trying to escape from our own fears or our own sins.

One almost wishes he had been in prison so he could talk as Peter and Paul did and have angels come, or as Alma and Amulek did and have the prison walls crumble, or as Joseph Smith did, a prophet who could write what may be the most sublime scriptural literature of our dispensation from the very center of a prison cell. I thank God that we live in such a time as we do, when the president and prophet of our church does not need to live in fear or imprisonment, and when we as a church are not required to go into bondage and into slavery. But there are other kinds of bonds and there are other kinds of prisons.

I believe with all my heart that if we can repent of our sins, if we can be charitable regarding the sins of others, if we can take courage toward our circumstances and try to do something about them, then there is a power, a living Father of us all who will reach down and "bear us as on eagles' wings." When Moses was called to lead the children of Israel out of Egypt, Jehovah said:

"The cry of the children of Israel is come unto me: and I have also seen the oppression wherewith the Egyptians oppress them. . . . I will send thee unto Pharaoh, that thou mayest bring forth my people the children of Israel out of Egypt. And Moses said unto God, who am I, that I should go unto Pharaoh . . . ? And he said, Certainly I will be with thee." (Exodus 3:9-12.)

And then there were demonstrations of God's commitment to freedom for his children. Sticks turned into serpents and water turned into blood, but that wasn't enough. There were plagues—frogs and lice, hail and locusts—and that wasn't enough. There was darkness, and finally there was death. Then the Israelites were set free from political servitude to pursue a higher freedom if they would. And that challenge remains before us.

Still stretching before you and me is something of a desert and a sea, like a barbed prison wire between our Egypt and our promised land. We're all somewhere in that desert. When that little band of Israelites gathered at the Mount of Sinai, Jehovah said to the sons of Abraham, "Thus shalt thou say to the house of Jacob, and tell the children of Israel; Ye have seen what I did unto the Egyptians, and how I bare you on eagles' wings, and brought you unto myself." (Exodus 19:3-4.)

In my life, I have been borne on eagles' wings. I know with all my heart that God lives, that Jesus is the Christ, that we will stand free for a time, unfettered and unencumbered, and that we will recognize in the marks on his flesh something of his bondage and imprisonment and dying service to us. I know that we must repent of our sins and that God has to be just, but

I also take great delight and eternal hope in the scriptural reassurance that where sin abounded, grace did much more abound and mercy claimeth the penitent.

6

A Robe, A Ring,
and a Fatted Calf

Perhaps the only thing worse than a mistake we might make is the greater mistake of not seeking forgiveness for it. Not only might we fail to seek Christ's forgiveness—the final and redeeming forgiveness that will save us—but too often we do not forgive ourselves and we do not forgive others. By dismissing the principles of repentance and forgiveness, we foolishly choose to make life more painful for ourselves and for those who truly need our help.

Recently I was invited to address the nearly two thousand missionaries in residence at the Missionary Training Center. Following my talk, several missionaries came up to visit briefly and discuss my message. I visited with many of them, and the minutes stretched into many minutes and then finally into nearly an hour. During that time I noticed one young elder hanging around the outer rim of the circle as all the other missionaries came and went.

Finally the traffic thinned out, and he stepped forward. "Do you remember me?" he asked.

"No," I said, "I'm sorry I don't. Tell me your name."

He replied, "My name is Elder _____." His eyes searched mine for recognition, but I just didn't know who the young man was.

Summoning his courage for the ultimate revelation, he

said, "Helaman Halls—A Faithful Friend Is a Strong Defense." Then I knew who he was. That little coded phrase may not ring any bells for you, but it meant something to him, and he knew it meant something to me.

On September 7, 1982, I gave the only angry public spanking I have ever given a group of BYU students. The title of my remarks for that back-to-school message was "A Faithful Friend Is a Strong Defense." I spoke of an offense, a felony—falsifying government documents—which had been committed in one of our residence halls the April before and had been widely covered by the press. Five months had passed but I was still hurting. Time had not soothed me.

I spoke of that incident publicly—without mentioning the names of the participants—because I care about matters of morality and honor and personal virtue at BYU. I wanted it clear that the behavior of every student at Brigham Young University matters very much to me and to what this school stands for. So I said my piece and, for all intents and purposes, forgot about it.

But it was not easy for the students involved. Not only were there the burdens of university and church actions, but the civil law made an indelible stroke across the record of some of these young lives. There were tears and courts and sentences and probations. Legally it had been about as much of a nightmare as a college freshman could have foreseen. Obviously it was *more* of a nightmare than they could have foreseen because the sorrow and remorse over their "prank"—I put the word in quotation marks—was deep and rending.

I recall that very unsavory experience simply to put a happy ending on one young man's very difficult experience. His father wrote me later and said how much courage it had taken for him to come up and talk with me at the MTC, but he said his son wanted me to know of his effort to make things right. It had not been easy for him to get a mission call. Not only were there all the court-imposed sanctions and church restrictions, but there was the terrible personal burden of guilt. But he wanted to serve a mission both because it was the right thing to do and because it was a way for him to say to the Church, the government, the university, and all who cared about him, "I'm back. I made a serious mistake but I'm back. I am making up lost ground. I've still got a chance."

There are other painful stories all around us about transgressions and heartache, stories involving very serious but usually less public mistakes. To those who are burdened with such problems, the redeeming love of Christ is available. His gospel is indeed the "good news." Because of him, we can rise above past problems, blot them out, and watch them die, if we are willing to have it so.

I am not sure what your most painful memories might be. I'm certain there are lots of problems we could all list. Some may be sins among the most serious God himself has listed. Others may be less serious disappointments, including a poor start in school, or a difficult relationship with your family, or personal pain with a friend. Whatever the list, it's bound to be long when we add up all the dumb things we've done. And my greatest fear is that we will not believe in other chances, that we will not understand repentance, that on some days we will not believe in any future at all.

In what may well be literature's most extreme and chilling observation of such debilitating, unassuaged guilt, we watch Macbeth—cousin of the king, masterful, strong, honored, and honorable—descend through a horrible series of bloody deeds by which his very soul is increasingly "tortured by an agony which [knows no] . . . repose." (A. C. Bradley, *Shakespearean Tragedy*, New York: Fawcett, 1967, p. 276.) Shapes of terror appear before his eyes, and the sounds of hell clamor in his ears.

His guilty heart and tormented conscience are shared by Lady Macbeth, and she too despairs. Undoubtedly reflecting

his own state of mind, Macbeth speaks to the physician about
his wife's circumstance:

> Canst thou not minister to a mind diseas'd,
> Pluck from the memory a rooted sorrow,
> Raze out the written troubles of the brain,
> And with some sweet oblivious antidote
> Cleanse the stuff'd bosom of that perilous stuff
> Which weighs upon the heart?

The doctor shakes his head over such diseases of the soul,
and says:

> Therein the patient
> Must minister to himself.

But the anguish of both man and wife continues unabated
until Macbeth says on the day he will die:

> Out, out, brief candle!
> Life's but a walking shadow, a poor player
> That struts and frets his hour upon the stage,
> And then is heard no more. It is a tale
> Told by an idiot, full of sound and fury,
> Signifying nothing.

Macbeth's murders are sins too strong for the kind of transgression in which you and I might be involved. But I believe
the despair of his final hopelessness can be applied at least in
part to our own circumstances. Unless we believe in repentance and restoration; unless we believe there can be a way
back from our mistakes, whether those sins be sexual or social
or civil or academic, whether they be great or small; unless
we believe we can start over on solid ground with our past put
behind us and genuine hope for the future—in short, unless
we believe in the compassion of Christ and his redemptive

love, then I think we in our own way are as hopeless as Macbeth and our view of life just as depressing. We do become shadows, feeble players on a perverse stage, in a tale told by an idiot. And unfortunately, in such a burdened state, we are the idiots.

As he began to write of what he would call the "miracle of forgiveness," President Kimball said:

> I had made up my mind that I would never write a book [but] . . . when I come in contact almost daily with broken homes, delinquent children, corrupt governments, and apostate groups, and realize that all these problems are the result of sin, I want to shout with Alma: "O . . . that I might go forth . . . with a voice to shake the earth, and cry repentance unto every people." (Al. 29:1.)
>
> Hence this book indicates the seriousness of breaking God's commandments; shows that sin can bring only sorrow, remorse, disappointment, and anguish; and warns that the small indiscretions evolve into larger ones and finally into major transgressions which bring heavy penalties. . . .
>
> [But] having come to recognize their deep sin, many have tended to surrender hope, not having a clear knowledge of the scriptures and of the redeeming power of Christ.
>
> [So I also] write to make the joyous affirmation that man can be literally transformed by his own repentance and by God's gift of forgiveness. . . .
>
> It is my humble hope that . . . [those] who are suffering the baleful effects of sin may be helped to find the way from darkness to light, from suffering to peace, from misery to hope, and from spiritual death to eternal life. (Preface, *The Miracle of Forgiveness*, Salt Lake City: Bookcraft, 1969, pp. x-xii.)

One of the added tragedies in transgression is that even if *we* make the effort to change, to try again, to come back, others often insist upon leaving the old labels with us.

I once knew a boy who had no father and precious few of

the other blessings of life. The young men in his community found it easy to tease and taunt and bully him. And in the process of it all he made some mistakes, though I cannot believe his mistakes were more serious than those of his Latter-day Saint friends who made life so miserable for him. He began to drink and smoke, and gospel principles that had never meant much to him now meant even less. He had been cast in a role by Latter-day Saint friends who should have known better, and he began to play the part perfectly. Soon he drank even more, went to school even less, and went to church not at all. Then one day he was gone. Some said they thought he had joined the army.

That was about 1959 or so. Fifteen or sixteen years later he came home. At least he tried to come home. He had found the significance of the gospel in his life. He had married a wonderful girl, and they had a beautiful family. But he discovered something upon his return. He had changed, but some of his old friends hadn't—and they were unwilling to let him escape his past.

This was hard for him and hard for his family. They bought a little home and started a small business, but they struggled both personally and professionally and finally moved away. For reasons that don't need to be detailed here, the story goes on to a very unhappy ending. He died not long after, at age forty-four. That's too young to die these days, and it's certainly too young to die away from home.

When a battered, weary swimmer tries valiantly to get back to shore after having fought strong winds and rough waves that he should never have challenged in the first place, those of us who might have had better judgment (or perhaps just better luck) ought not to row out to his side, beat him with our oars, and shove his head back underwater. That's not what boats were made for. But some of us do that to each other.

In general conference a few years ago Elder David B. Haight told us that—

Arturo Toscanini, the late, famous conductor of the New York Philharmonic Orchestra, received a brief, crumpled letter from a lonely sheepherder in the remote mountain area of Wyoming:

"Mr. Conductor: I have only two possessions—a radio and an old violin. The batteries in my radio are getting low and will soon die. My violin is so out of tune I can't use it. Please help me. Next Sunday when you begin your concert, sound a loud 'A' so I can tune my 'A' string; then I can tune the other strings. When my radio batteries are dead, I'll have my violin."

At the beginning of his next nationwide radio concert from Carnegie Hall, Toscanini announced: "For a dear friend and listener back in the mountains of Wyoming the orchestra will now sound an 'A.'" The musicians all joined together in a perfect "A."

The lonely sheepherder only needed one note, just a little help to get back in tune; . . . he needed someone who cared to assist him with one string; [after that] the others would be easy. ("People to People," *Ensign*, November 1981, p. 54.)

In the early years of the Church the Prophet Joseph Smith had no more faithful aide than William Wines Phelps. Brother Phelps, a former newspaper editor, had joined the Church in Kirtland and was of such assistance to those early leaders that they sent him as one of the first Latter-day Saints to the new Jerusalem—Jackson County, Missouri. There he was called by the Lord to the stake presidency of that "center stake of Zion."

But then troubles developed. First they were largely ecclesiastical aberrations but later there were financial improprieties. Things became so serious that the Lord revealed to Joseph Smith that if Brother Phelps did not repent, he would be "removed out of [his] place." (HC 2:511.) He did not repent, and he was excommunicated on March 10, 1838.

The Prophet Joseph and others immediately tried to love W. W. Phelps back into the fold, but he would have nothing of it. Then in the fall of that violent year Brother Phelps, along with others, signed a deadly, damaging affidavit against the Prophet and other leaders of the Church. The result was quite simply that Joseph Smith was sentenced to be publicly executed on the town square in Far West, Missouri, Friday morning, November 2, 1838. Through the monumental courage of General Alexander Doniphan, the Prophet was miraculously spared the execution W. W. Phelps and others had precipitated, but he was not spared spending five months—November through April—in several Missouri prisons, the most noted of which was the pit known ironically as Liberty jail.

I do not need to recount for you the suffering of the Saints through that period. The anguish of those not captive was in many ways more severe than those imprisoned. The persecution intensified until the Saints sought yet again to find another refuge from the storm. With Joseph in chains, praying for their safety and giving some direction by letter, they made their way toward Commerce, Illinois, a malaria swamp on the Mississippi River where they would try once more to build the City of Zion. And much of this travail, this torment and heartache, was due to men of their own brotherhood like W. W. Phelps.

But we're speaking of happy endings. Two very difficult years later, with great anguish and remorse of conscience, William Phelps wrote to Joseph Smith in Nauvoo.

> Brother Joseph: . . . I am as the prodigal son. . . .
>
> I have seen the folly of my way, and I tremble at the gulf I have passed. . . . [I] ask my old brethren to forgive me, and though they chasten me to death, yet I will die with them, for their God is my God. The least place with them is enough for me, yea, it is bigger and better than all Babylon. . . .
>
> I know my situation, you know it, and God knows it, and I want to be saved if my friends will help me. . . . I have done wrong and I am sorry. . . . I ask forgiveness. . . . I

want your fellowship; if you cannot grant that, grant me your peace and friendship, for we are brethren, and our communion used to be sweet. (HC 4:141-42.)

In an instant the Prophet wrote back. I know of no private document or personal response in the life of Joseph Smith—or anyone else, for that matter—that so powerfully demonstrates the magnificence of his soul. There is a lesson here for every one of us who claims to be a disciple of Christ. He wrote:

Dear Brother Phelps: . . . You may in some measure realize what my feelings . . . were, when we read your letter. . . . We have suffered much in consequence of your behavior—the cup of gall, already full enough for mortals to drink, was indeed filled to overflowing when you turned against us. . . .

However, the cup has been drunk, the will of our Father has been done, and we are yet alive, for which we thank the Lord. And having been delivered from the hands of wicked men by the mercy of our God, we say it is your privilege to be delivered from the powers of the adversary, be brought into the liberty of God's dear children, and again take your stand among the Saints of the Most High, and by diligence, humility, and love unfeigned, commend yourself to our God, and your God, and to the Church of Jesus Christ.

Believing your confession to be real, and your repentance genuine, I shall be happy once again to give you the right hand of fellowship, and rejoice over the returning prodigal. . . .

"Come on, dear brother, since the war is past,
For friends at first, are friends again at last."
　　　　　Yours as ever,
　　　　　　Joseph Smith, Jun. (HC 4:162-64.)

It only adds to the poignance of this particular prodigal's return that exactly four years later—almost to the day—it would be W. W. Phelps selected to preach Joseph Smith's funeral sermon in that terribly tense and emotional circumstance. Furthermore it would be W. W. Phelps who would memorialize the martyred prophet with his hymn of adoration, "Praise to the Man." (*Hymns*, no. 147.)

Having been the foolish swimmer pulled back to safety by the very man he had sought to destroy, Brother Phelps must have had unique appreciation for the stature of the Prophet when he penned:

> Great is his glory and endless his priesthood.
> Ever and ever the keys he will hold.
> Faithful and true, he will enter his kingdom,
> Crowned in the midst of the prophets of old.

Next time you sing that hymn, remember what it meant to W. W. Phelps to be given another chance.

One of the most encouraging and compassionate parables in all of Holy Writ is the story of the prodigal son. Mary Lyman Henrie's poetic expression of it is entitled "To Any Who Have Watched for a Son's Returning."

> He watched his son gather all the goods
> that were his lot,
> anxious to be gone from tending flocks,
> the dullness of the fields.
> He stood by the olive tree gate long
> after the caravan disappeared
> where the road climbs the hills
> on the far side of the valley,
> into infinity.
> Through changing seasons he spent the light
> in a great chair, facing the far country,
> and that speck of road on the horizon.
> Mocking friends: "He will not come."
> Whispering servants: "The old man
> has lost his senses."
> A chiding son: "You should not have let him go."

A grieving wife: "You need rest and sleep."
She covered his drooping shoulders,
his callused knees, when east winds blew chill, until that
day . . .
A form familiar, even at infinity,
in shreds, alone, stumbling over pebbles.
"When he was a great way off,
His father saw him,
and had compassion, and ran,
and fell on his neck, and kissed him." (Luke 15:20.)
(*Ensign*, March 1983, p. 63. Used by permission.)

God bless us to help each other come back home, where
we will, in the presence of our Father, find waiting a robe, a
ring, and a fatted calf.

7

Born of God:
Alma, Son of Alma

Forgiveness and the chance to change our past is at the heart of Christ's greatest gift to us all: the atoning sacrifice so willingly begun in Gethsemane and concluded upon the cross of Calvary. We "all have sinned and come short of the glory of God," so we take courage when we see the repentance of one like young Alma, who changed his life as dramatically and instantly as any man ever has. To be born of God is to find "marvelous light . . . and exquisite joy."

There are multitudes of men and women—in and out of the Church—who are struggling vainly against obstacles in their path. Many are fighting the battle of life—and losing. Indeed, there are those among us who consider themselves the vilest of sinners.

We have all known such people. We have all spoken with someone who does not think he has been forgiven—or worse, who does not think he can be forgiven. How many broken hearts remain broken because those people feel they are beyond the pale of God's restorative power? How many bruised and battered spirits are certain that they have sunk to a depth at which the light of redeeming hope and grace will never again shine?

To these, the story of the younger Alma comes like water to a parched tongue, like rest to a weary traveler. From the depths of hellish iniquity, from rebellion and destruction and utter wickedness, the younger Alma returned—and therein lies again the "miracle of forgiveness." It *is* a miracle. In fact, it is the greatest of all miracles. It is the miracle at the heart of the atonement of Jesus Christ.

Surely that is the "good news" of the gospel—that there is a way back, that there is repentance and safety and peace because of Christ's gift to us. The good news is that the nightmares—large ones, little ones, every fear and concern—can end, and a safe loving light can shine in that "dark place, until the day dawn[s]," clean and clear and gloriously bright, and "the day star arise[s] in [our] hearts." (2 Peter 1:19.)

That is the message all the world must hear.

The process of repenting, of course, is not an easy one. The experience of young Alma is a frightening testament of that. Wrongs must be made right, and there is no painless way to accomplish it. But it must be done, and with Alma, we can all thank our Heavenly Father that it can be done. However weary or wicked we may feel, the story of the younger Alma is an open invitation to every child of God. It is the promise that, with the psalmist, we too may sing:

"The Lord is my shepherd; I shall not want. . . . He restoreth my soul. . . . Yea, though I walk through the valley of the shadow of death, I will fear no evil. . . . Surely goodness and mercy shall follow me all the days of my life: and I will dwell in the house of the Lord for ever." (Psalm 23.)

The sons of strong fathers provide many of the messages in the Book of Mormon. Nephi and Jacob, sons of Lehi, recorded almost all of the material given on the small plates of Nephi. Moroni, son of Mormon, concluded his father's work and some fourteen hundred years later delivered it to the young prophet Joseph Smith. Other sons who learned great lessons from their parents provide commentary throughout this sacred scripture.

Perhaps no son, however, captures our imagination like the younger Alma. More pages are devoted to the span of his life and ministry than to any other person in the Book of Mormon, and the book that bears his name is nearly two and a half times longer than any other in the record. He strides with prophetic power onto the great center stage of the Book of Mormon, appearing near the precise chronological midpoint of the record—five hundred years after Lehi leaves Jerusalem, five hundred years before Moroni seals up the record.

The centrality of Alma's life is not limited simply to chronology or pagination, however. The significance of his life is in the course that it took. The gospel of Christ is literally "the glad tidings . . . that he came into the world, even Jesus, to be crucified for the world, and to bear the sins of the world, and to sanctify the world, and to cleanse it from all unrighteousness; that through him all might be saved." (D&C 76:40-42.)

The life of the younger Alma portrays the gospel's beauty and reach and power perhaps more than any other in holy scripture. Such dramatic redemption and movement away from wickedness and toward the permanent joy of exaltation may not be outlined with more compelling force anywhere else. In him is symbolized the task of the whole human family, which must, as Paul commands, "leave your former way of life, . . . lay aside that old human nature which, deluded by its lusts, is sinking towards death. You must be made new in mind and spirit, and put on the new nature." (Ephesians 4:22-24, New English Bible.)

The first mention of young Alma tells us of a difficult time. (Mosiah 27:8.) We might wish to know more of the causes for such difficulties, but we are told little of his early life. Was he born in the land of Nephi? If so, was it before or after his father's conversion? Or was he born in Zarahemla, in the presence of third- and fourth-generation Christians? What training did he have? Who influenced him? What were his hopes and fears and aspirations?

We do not have the answers to these questions, but we

know something went very, very wrong. Unlike most other father and son relationships noted in the Book of Mormon, the bond between the two Almas is characterized, when we first learn of it, by anguish and opposition. The elder Alma had not been born into church activity, and had it not been for the dramatic message of Abinadi before the court of Noah, perhaps the light of the gospel would never have penetrated the darkness of his world.

But that light had come, and Alma the Elder immediately chose to walk by it. He began to build the church despite the threat of danger to his own life and the lives of those who followed him. With great difficulty he led his little group of followers out of the then-apostate land of Nephi and established them with the faithful body of the church in Zarahemla. (See Mosiah 23–25.) Surely only those who have paid such a price for the gospel can appreciate what deep meaning the church has in their lives. Of course, the emotion of that commitment is often intensified when others do not recognize that same meaning or sense the same importance. So it was with the elder Alma. As he now directed the affairs of the church in Zarahemla (see Mosiah 26:8), he found that "there were many of the rising generation that . . . did not believe the tradition of their fathers. . . . And now because of their unbelief they could not understand the word of God; and their hearts were hardened. And they would not be baptized; neither would they join the church. And they were a separate people as to their faith, and remained so ever after, even in their carnal and sinful state; for they would not call upon the Lord their God." (Mosiah 26:1, 3-4.)

This group brought great difficulty and deep heartache to the elder Alma, and he was "troubled in his spirit." (Mosiah 26:10.) He labored faithfully, however, inviting such young people to repent as he himself had done. Some did number themselves among the people of God. Others, however, "would not confess their sins and repent of their iniquity"

(Mosiah 26:36), and the names of these were stricken from the records of the church.

An ecclesiastical problem became a personal tragedy when the elder Alma found that his own son, "called Alma, after his father," was numbered among these unbelievers. Perhaps no anguish of the human spirit matches the anguish of a mother or father who fears for the soul of a child. Through this travail the elder Alma, and undoubtedly his beloved wife, waded—and waited. We do not know how sinful the young Alma really was, but the scripture records he was "a very wicked and an idolatrous man" (Mosiah 27:8), who, with the sons of Mosiah, was "the very vilest of sinners" (Mosiah 28:4). We know he conscientiously worked at destroying the church of God, "stealing away the hearts of the people" and causing dissension among them. (Mosiah 27:9.) He was in every way "a great hinderment to the prosperity of the church of God." (Mosiah 27:9.)

Years later, the younger Alma recounted these events in order to save his own sons from walking such a painful path: "I had rebelled against my God, and . . . had not kept his holy commandments. Yea, and I had murdered many of his children, or rather led them away unto destruction; yea, . . . so great had been my iniquities, that the very thought of coming into the presence of my God did rack my soul with inexpressible horror." (Alma 36:13-14.)

Yet Alma returned from such terrible sin and its consequences to become a noble example of faith, service, and righteousness. How did he do it? Can we do it? What can we learn?

We learn that there is majestic, undeniable power in the love and prayer of a parent. The angel who appeared to Alma and the sons of Mosiah did not come in response to any righteousness on their part, though their souls were still precious in the sight of God. He came in response to the prayers of a faithful parent. "The Lord hath heard the prayers . . . of his servant, Alma, who is thy father," declared the angel with a voice of thunder that shook the earth, "for he has prayed with much faith concerning thee that thou mightest be brought to the knowledge of the truth; therefore, for this purpose have I come to convince thee of the power and authority of God, that the prayers of his servants might be answered according to their faith." (Mosiah 27:14.)

Parental prayer is an unfathomable source of power. Parents can never give up hoping or caring or believing. Surely they can never give up praying. At times prayer may be the only course of action remaining—but it is the most powerful of them all.

We learn that there is great power in the united faith of the priesthood. It was not only the elder Alma who prayed when his son was laid helpless and insensible before him, but also the priests and, we might assume, other faithful friends and neighbors. With the support of more private prayers, the priesthood assembled and "began to fast, and to pray to the Lord their God that he would open the mouth of Alma, that he might speak, and also that his limbs might receive their strength—that the eyes of the people might be opened to see and know of the goodness and glory of God." (Mosiah 27:22.)

Here is a majestic example of Christlike love. No one in this group seemed delighted that devastating recompense had finally come. No one here seemed pleased to imagine the torment of this young spirit. Yet this was the young man who had despised their faith, harmed their lives, and attempted to destroy the very church of God, which they held dearer than life itself. But their response was the response of the Master: "Love your enemies, bless them that curse you, do good to them that hate you, and *pray for them which despitefully use you,* and persecute you." (Matthew 5:44. Italics added.) These saints were wise enough to know that they and every other human soul are wholly dependent on the merciful gift of God's forgiveness, "for all have sinned, and come short of the glory of God." (Romans 3:23.) What we all need, we cannot in good conscience or integrity deny another. So they prayed for him who had despitefully used them.

We learn that repentance is a very painful process. By his own admission Alma said he wandered "through much tribulation, repenting nigh unto death," that he was consumed with an "everlasting burning. . . . I was in the darkest abyss," he said. "My soul was racked with eternal torment." (Mosiah 27:28-29.)

"My soul was harrowed up to the greatest degree and racked with all my sins. . . . I was tormented with the pains of hell. . . . The very thought of coming into the presence of my God did rack my soul with inexpressible horror." Then this most appalling cry: "Oh, thought I, that I could be banished and become extinct both soul and body, that I might not be brought to stand in the presence of my God, to be judged of my deeds." (Alma 36:12-15.)

For three seemingly endless days and nights he was torn "with the pains of a damned soul" (Alma 36:16), pain so real that he was physically incapacitated and spiritually terrorized by what appeared to be his ultimate fate. No one should think that the gift of forgiveness is fully realized without significant effort on the part of the forgiven. No one should be foolish enough to sin willingly or wantonly, thinking forgiveness is easily available.

Repentance of necessity involves suffering and sorrow. Anyone who thinks otherwise has not read the life of the young Alma, nor tried personally to repent. In the process of repentance we are granted just a taste of the suffering we would endure if we failed to turn away from evil. That pain, though only momentary for the repentant, is the most bitter of cups. No man or woman should be foolish enough to think it can be sipped, even briefly, without consequence. Remember the words of the Son of God himself of those who don't repent: "Therefore I command you to repent—repent, lest I smite you by the rod of my mouth, and by my wrath, and by my anger, and your sufferings be sore—how sore you know not, how exquisite you know not, yea, how hard to bear you know not. . . . Which suffering caused myself, even God, the greatest of all, to tremble because of pain, and to bleed at every pore, and to suffer both body and spirit—and would that I might not drink the bitter cup, and shrink." (D&C 19:15, 18.)

We learn that when repentance is complete, we are born again and leave behind forever the self we once were. To me, none of the many approaches to teaching repentance falls more short than the well-intentioned suggestion that "although a nail may be removed from a wooden post, there will forever be a hole in that post." We know that repentance (the removal of that nail, if you will) can be a very long and painful and difficult task. Unfortunately, some will never have the incentive to undertake it. We even know that there are a very few sins for which no repentance is possible. But where repentance *is* possible, and its requirements are faithfully pursued and completed, there is no "hole left in the post" for the bold reason that it is no longer the same post. It is a new post. We can start again, utterly clean, with a new will and a new way of life.

Through repentance, we are changed to what Alma calls "new creatures." (Mosiah 27:26.) We are "born again; yea, born of God, changed from [our] carnal and fallen state, to a state of righteousness, being redeemed of God, becoming his sons and daughters." (Mosiah 27:25; see also 5:1-12.) Repentance and baptism allow Christ to purify our lives in the blood of the Lamb and we are clean again. What we were, we never have to be again, for God in his mercy has promised that "he who has repented of his sins, the same is forgiven, and I, the Lord, remember them no more." (D&C 58:42.)

We learn that the teachings and testimonies of parents and other good people have an inevitable, inexorable effect. Those lessons are not lost on even the most wayward soul. Somewhere, somehow, they get recorded in the soul and may be called upon in a great moment of need. It was in such a moment that the young Alma "remembered also to have heard my father prophesy." (Alma 36:17.) That prophecy may have been uttered in a day when Alma was taunting his father, or jeering at those who believed, or willfully denying the reality of revelation. It may have come at a time when his father assumed Alma did not care or hear or understand. Or it may have come so early in life that his father might think he had forgotten. We do not know when the lesson was taught. But somewhere, sometime, one or more or a dozen of those teachings had been heard and had been implanted somewhere in his heart. Now it was being called forth for the very protection it had intended to give. Like Enos, who was haunted by "the words which I had often heard my father speak" (Enos 1:3), Alma also remembered—and believed. Parents, friends, teachers—none must ever stop teaching and testifying. There will always be great power—even latent, delayed, residual power—in the words of God we utter.

We learn above all else that Christ is the power behind all repentance. We have noted above that Alma had been touched by the teaching of his father, but it is particularly important that the prophecy he remembered was one regarding "the coming of one Jesus Christ, a Son of God, to atone for the sins of the world." (Alma 36:17.) That is the name and that is the message that every person must hear. Alma heard it, and he cried out from the anguish of a hell that kept burning and a conscience that wouldn't heal, "O Jesus, thou Son of God, have mercy on me." (Alma 36:18.) Perhaps such a prayer, though brief, is the most significant one that can be uttered in this world. Whatever other prayers we offer, whatever other needs we have, all somehow depends on that plea: "O Jesus, thou Son of God, have mercy on me." He is prepared to provide that mercy. He paid with his very life in order to give it. The least we can do is ask for it and be worthy of it and love it and appreciate the magnitude of its meaning. "There is none other name under heaven given among men, whereby we must be saved." (Acts 4:12.)

If Alma's may be the central *human* story in the Book of Mormon, surely Christ's is the central name to the story within the story. It is in exactly this way that the Book of Mormon testifies that Jesus is the Christ—not only in terms of theology and doctrine and precept, which are important, but also in the very power of his name, the reality of his life, and the reach of his priesthood, which are even more important.

We learn, then, that through repentance the earlier sorrow and darkness are transformed into joy and light. Calling out to Christ for salvation from the gall of bitterness and the everlasting chains of death, Alma found his pain being lifted. Replacing it were peace and new possibilities. "And oh, what joy, and what marvelous light I did behold; yea, my soul was filled with joy as exceeding as was my pain! . . . There can be nothing so exquisite and sweet as was my joy." (Alma 36:20-21.)

With that wonderful transformation comes another intriguing, even more revealing, change. This young man who was so tormented and horrified at the thought of coming back into the presence of God—who literally wished to be annihilated so he would not have to face the great Judge of the quick and the dead—now has opened to him a vision of God sitting upon his throne, and with his newly cleansed soul he cries, "My soul did long to be there." (Alma 36:22.)

Not only does our spiritual record change and our physical life become clean, but also our very desires are purified and made whole. Our will quite literally changes to receive *His* will. We may have avoided church attendance, the sacrament, the bishop, our parents, our worthy companions—avoided anyone we had sinned against, including God himself—but now that repentant heart longs to be with them. That is part of the joy and light of the Atonement—the "at-one-ment"—which not only binds us back to God but also brings us back to a special unity with our best natural self and our most beloved human associates.

We learn last of all that the ultimate proof of our repentance is in its permanence. (See D&C 58:43.) Its blessings should be in our memories constantly, compelling us to continue in the cause of truth and to lend our best efforts to the work of God. Alma's testimony is that from the very hour of his conversion "until now, I have labored without ceasing, that I might bring souls unto repentance; that I might bring them to taste of the exceeding joy of which I did taste; that they might also be born of God, and be filled with the Holy Ghost. . . .

"Because of the word which he has imparted unto me, behold, many have been born of God, and have tasted as I have tasted, and have seen eye to eye as I have seen; therefore they do know of these things of which I have spoken, as I do know; and the knowledge which I have is of God. And I have been supported under trials and troubles of every kind, yea, and in all manner of afflictions; yea, God has delivered me from prison, and from bonds, and from death; yea, and I do put my trust in him, and he will still deliver me. And I know that he will raise me up at the last day, to dwell with him in glory; yea, and I will praise him forever." (Alma 36:24, 26-28.)

And so he lived. From the depths of sin Alma repented and became a prophetic model of virtue and valor, becoming one of the greatest missionaries of any dispensation of the world. There is so much that should be said of him: his political role, his high priestly power, his missionary trials, his concern for his own sons. He saw people repent at great social and political cost. Some paid with their very lives. He met others, even antichrists, who would not repent, and he testified boldly against them. He saw faith as a seed that will grow if we nourish it, and he wished he were an angel that all could hear his word. He taught deep doctrines, he lived by sublime personal values, and he rejoiced in his own missionary success and the success of his brethren. But these all came after (and finally only because of) his willingness to undergo what one twentieth-century writer has called "the ordeal of change": movement from night to day, from pain to peace, from sin to the joy of salvation—that monumental process of the soul called repentance.

"O Jesus, thou Son of God, have mercy on me" is the cry that changed Alma's world forever. Then one day he was taken home. He left to join his brethren, men like Adam, Abraham, Nephi, and Jacob. But surely he went first to seek the companionship of his Savior, who had made it all possible and so perfect. After a long and beautiful life of service, the great desire of his soul was finally granted to him: he "did long to be there" with his Master. Perhaps no personal journey gives more encouragement to you or me that peace and joy are possible, that it can—and must—be so.

8

The Lengthening Shadow
of Peter

So often we feel we are the only ones who have ever been tried or tempted. We forget that Christ himself was tempted and that so were his apostles and prophets. Peter's life shows the developing faith of a magnificent soul, including his progressive ability to face and resolve difficult problems. His story is an important reminder that our whole life is what counts, that God's "grace is sufficient for the meek," and that he does "make weak things become strong."

Several years ago a newspaper carried an Easter Sunday editorial written by a minister of religion. The editorial lamented the career of the apostle Peter, denouncing among other things his indecisiveness, lack of humility, fear of man, and failure to pray. The minister concluded his Easter appeal: "Let us as people, especially those who are Christians and claim to abide by the Word of God, not make the same mistakes and fall as Peter fell."

This editorial came to the attention of another "Peter," another resolute chief apostle. President Spencer W. Kimball, then Acting President of the Quorum of the Twelve, saw this journalistic piece and shuddered.

"I had some strange emotions," he recounted before an audience of young adults. "I was shocked, then I was chilled, then my blood changed its temperature and began to boil. I felt

I was attacked viciously, for Peter was my brother, my colleague, my example, my prophet, and God's anointed. I whispered to myself, 'That is not true. He is maligning my brother.'" ("Peter, My Brother," BYU *Speeches of the Year*, July 13, 1971.)

Move from this scene of one mighty apostle defending another to a scene in Jerusalem not long after Jesus' ascension into heaven. Peter and John were about to enter the temple to worship and seek strength for the tasks that lay before them. A forty-year-old man, "lame from his mother's womb," asked alms of them as they passed. There was nothing unique about his plea; the man had been begging every day for years in this same place. But Peter did not brush by. What would his petition mean, offered up in this holy house at the hour of prayer, if he suffered this man to offer up a similar petition in vain?

He turned to the invalid, "fastening his eyes on him" with a gaze that probed the deepest recesses of his soul. Finding faith there, Peter said deliberately and clear: "Silver and gold have I none; but such as I have give I thee: In the name of Jesus Christ of Nazareth rise up and walk." (Acts 3:1-6.) Peter had no money but he had riches. "Such as he had" included every key of the kingdom of God on earth, priesthood power to raise the dead, faith to strengthen bones and sinews, a strong right hand of Christian fellowship. He could not give silver or gold, but he could give that which is always purchased "without money and without price" (Isaiah 55:1)—and he gave it.

President Harold B. Lee, who loved this powerful account of the priesthood in action, once said, "Now in my mind's eye I can picture this [lame] man and what was in his mind. 'Doesn't this man know I have never walked? He commands me to walk.' But the biblical record doesn't end there. Peter just didn't content himself by commanding the man to walk, but he 'took him by the right hand, and lifted him up. . . .'

"Will you see that picture now of that noble soul," invited President Lee, "that chiefest of the apostles, perhaps with his arms around the shoulders of the man, and saying, 'Now, my good man, have courage. I will take a few steps with you. Let's walk together. . . .' Then the man leaped with joy.

"You cannot lift another soul until you are standing on higher ground than he is," President Lee concluded. "You must be sure, if you would rescue the man, that you yourself are setting the example of what you would have him be. You cannot light a fire in another soul unless it is burning in your own." (*Stand Ye in Holy Places,* Deseret Book, 1974, pp. 186-87.)

Who was this man among men, admired by modern prophets and anointed of God? What manner of man is chosen from among the host of heaven to become the first ordained apostle of the Lord Jesus Christ and lead His church in perilous times? How high was the ground he stood on? How bright was the fire in his soul? For answers, we open the scriptures and find "a man who had grown perfect through his experiences and sufferings—a man with vision, a man of revelations, a man fully trusted by his Lord Jesus Christ." (Kimball, *op. cit.*) We find there a mighty stone in Israel.

When Jesus walked out of the wilderness after forty days and nights of preparation, his eye fell upon a man who made his living sailing on a turbulent sea. With powers of discernment not of this world, he declared in that first encounter, "Thou art Simon, the son of Jona: thou shalt be called Cephas," or literally, a stone or rock. (John 1:42.)

Here was a principal building block for the priestly foundation to be laid. Jesus himself would be the chief cornerstone, but at his side would be apostles and prophets full of courage and strength and integrity. In those earliest hours of his ministry, Jesus had found the man prepared from before the foundation of the world to become his chief apostle and special witness in the dispensation of the meridian of time.

Peter was, in President Kimball's words, "a diamond in the rough—a diamond that would need to be cut, trimmed, and polished by correction, chastisement, and trials—but nevertheless a diamond of real quality. The Savior knew this apostle could be trusted to receive the keys of the kingdom." Time was short. Much had to be done in a matter of months. Jesus prepared Peter as quickly as possible for the call that was to come.

"Launch out into the deep," he counseled this fisherman one morning in Galilee, "and let down your nets for a draught." After an unsuccessful night of effort, Peter's judgment told him a final effort was useless. But this was a man of genuinely childlike faith, and he lowered the net. The number of fish taken in that single attempt strained the strings until they began to break, and filled two boats until they began to sink. In that small ship Peter, stunned, kneeled at the feet of the Master. Jesus said lovingly, "Henceforth thou shalt catch men."

Launch out into the deep! Peter could not have known the ever-widening circles that single command would make in the stream of his plain and simple life. He was launching out into the expanse of godliness, into the eternal possibilities of redeemed and celestial life. He would be learning the mysteries of the kingdom. He would be hearing unspeakable things. To launch out into that limitless sea of the gospel of Jesus Christ, Peter brought his craft to shore, turned his back on the most spectacular single catch ever taken from Galilee, "forsook all, and followed him." (Luke 5:1-11.)

From that moment on, Jesus taught and trained Peter at every opportunity. He walked with him in the hills outside of Capernaum. He sat with him beside the sea they loved so much. He stayed in his home, ate at his table, gave blessings to his family and friends. Peter watched silently as the Son of God cast out devils, healed the sick, restored the blind. When Jesus sought some respite from the crowd, Peter appealed to him in their behalf. "All men seek for thee" (Mark 1:37), he told the Master, and Jesus smiled a knowing smile. Peter did not know that very soon other men would seek Jesus—and not to receive a blessing at his hand. But Jesus knew, and he hastened the work.

He called his disciples together, chose twelve from among them to be apostles, and ordained Peter to be the president of the council they now constituted. This newly appointed officer watched and learned and added to his faith, wholly absorbed in the life of his Teacher. He eagerly walked along the pathway of miracles Jesus walked, but slowed to stand in reverential wonder as the Redeemer took the lifeless hand of a child and commanded her to arise. Though Peter had never witnessed such an event nor imagined it could be so, nevertheless "her spirit came again, and she arose straightway." (Luke 8:55.)

Like Mary before him, so Peter must have kept all these things and pondered them in his heart. Little did he know that one day he would vividly recall every detail of this dramatic moment and, taking another beautiful girl by the hand, raise her from the dead. (Acts 9:40-41.)

As surely as the Jordan runs to its sea, this uniquely designed training had its calculated and inevitable effect. Peter's faith began to reach heights virtually without equal in the New Testament record. It so surged within him that upon the Lord's invitation, Peter once climbed down out of his fishing boat and "walked on the water, to go to Jesus." (Matthew 14:29.) That fact of faith has never been recorded of any other mortal man. If his faith faltered because of treacherous waves and adverse winds, "perhaps we should take a few steps on [the] water" before ascending to the judgment seat. (See Richard Lloyd Anderson, "Simon Peter," *Ensign*, February 1975, pp. 47-49.) In any case, with such rigorous challenges and "hard sayings" increasingly apparent in Jesus' teachings, many of the followers were unable to endure "and walked no more with him." But as the numbers dwindled, Peter was the more conspicuous by his presence. He knew no other way. He believed and so declared, "Lord, . . . thou hast the words of eternal life." (John 6:60-69.)

Such increasing conviction soon found its most profound utterance on the road to Caesarea Philippi. When Jesus asked his disciples, "Whom say ye that I am?" Simon Peter could not be restrained. With a conviction born not of reason or signs but of undeniable revelation from God, Peter burst forth: "Thou art the Christ, the Son of the living God." (Matthew 16:15-16.) From the moment he had named Peter *Cephas,* Jesus had been waiting for this man's strength of testimony to equal his strength of character. That time had come, and Peter was ready to receive the remaining keys of the kingdom.

With Jesus leading the way, Peter, James and John ascended "an high mountain apart" and there witnessed the transfiguration of the Son of God. The Lord's face shone as brightly as the sun at noonday and his raiment was as radiant as light itself. Then heavenly messengers appeared, bestowing upon this First Presidency every needful key for their ministry. In benediction to the event, a bright cloud overshadowed them and they heard the voice of Deity declare, "This is my beloved Son, in whom I am well pleased; hear ye him." (Matthew 17:5.)

The moment passed. The vision ceased. Peter still had many lessons to learn in the days ahead—of political loyalty and personal forgiveness, of material sacrifice and fruitful service. With his brethren he was yet to receive the sacrament of the Lord's Supper, hear Jesus pray for their unity, and discover which of their number was "a devil." (John 6:70.) But whatever lay before him, the transfer of authority was now complete. Endowed with power from on high and armed with the certainty of his conviction, he descended with Jesus into the valley of the shadow of death.

Peter could not descend completely with Christ; no one could. Furthermore, he was restrained by Jesus himself when he physically assaulted those who had come to seize the Lord. Peter could not go with him, but neither could he in his most confused and frightened moment flee from him. Denying that he knew him, Peter stood in the courtyard of the accusers and saw the indignities his Lord and Savior suffered. Then he did what all repentant men have cause to do. Silently and alone, he "went out, and wept bitterly." (Luke 22:62.)

Peter had been certain that his strength was sufficient for such times; that if necessary he would withstand evil alone. Reassuringly he had said to Jesus, "Though all men shall be offended because of thee, yet will I never be offended." (Matthew 26:33.) But in the kingdom of God, no man's strength is sufficient. This sobering, sorrowing realization— that he was not, of himself, capable of what God requires—was perhaps the final ingredient in Peter's short months of personal preparation.

In the years ahead, Peter would preside over the Church of Jesus Christ with dignity and great power, not in spite of his need for divine assistance but clearly and admittedly because of it. Heavenly guidance and spiritual manifestation would be the marks of his administration. And there would never again be a denial of Jesus. "Why look ye so earnestly on us, as though by our own power or holiness we had made this man to walk?" he would declare to all who marveled at the miracles. "Jesus, whom ye delivered up, . . . his name . . . hath made this man strong." (Acts 3:12-16.)

Responding to the resurrected Lord's thrice-repeated injunction to "Feed my sheep," Peter took vigorous command of his assignment. Moving quickly to fill the vacancy created in the Twelve by the death of Judas, Peter and his brethren were prepared on the Day of Pentecost for the promised outpouring of the Spirit of the Lord. This fiftieth day after Passover had traditionally been celebrated in Israel as the "Feast of the Harvest" (Exodus 23:16) or "Day of the Firstfruits" (Numbers 28:26). Now it is remembered as the day the Lord sent with "cloven tongues like as of fire" his benefaction upon the church and the harvesting of souls about to begin. Indeed, it literally marked the firstfruits of Peter's missionary labors. So powerful was his witness of these manifest wonders of Christ that fully three thousand souls were "pricked in their heart" and accepted Peter's invitation to "Repent, and be baptized . . . in the name of Jesus Christ . . . and . . . receive the gift of the Holy Ghost." (Acts 2, *passim.*) Days later his message of "Repent ye therefore, and be converted" was heard in Jerusalem, and five thousand believed. (Acts 3:19; 4:4.) Sacred writ contains few accounts of missionary powers like these. Wherever Peter went, men and women heard a testimony kindled by the revelations of God.

Of course, the tidal wave of conversion that swept Jerusalem under Peter's direction aroused the anger and fear of both Sadducee and Pharisee. But Peter's compelling declarations could not be silenced. In prison he overwhelmed his accusers with a piercing testimony of Jesus and found himself set free by angels as well as mortal men. Such powers stunned Jewish lawyers, who marveled at these "unlearned and ignorant men." (Acts 4:13.) They did not understand that in the gospel of Jesus Christ those have never been synonymous terms.

The Spirit of the Lord attended the Twelve wherever they met, both shaking body and building with its power. Multitudes were brought to them, and they were healed "every one." (Acts 5:16.) Faith in Peter's faith brought the sick into the streets on their beds of affliction "that at least the shadow of Peter passing by might overshadow some of them." (Acts 5:15.) One wonders if there is a single written line in any other record that stands as a greater monument to the faith and power of one mortal man bearing the holy priesthood of God. May we be forgiven for accusations of "indecisiveness, lack of humility, fear of man, and failure to pray."

With his own sense of urgency, Peter aggressively defied the injunction not to teach in the name of Christ, and returned again and again to the temple, where his safety was never secure. President Kimball pictures him there in the

House of the Lord, "the number one man in all the world," stretching to his full height and speaking with power to those who could imprison him, flog him, even take his life from him. With "courage superior and integrity supreme" (Kimball, *Faith Precedes the Miracle,* p. 244), Peter testified plainly, "We ought to obey God rather than men. . . . We are his witnesses of these things." (Acts 5:29, 32.) Imprisoned and beaten, forbidden to speak, Peter was as irrepressible as Daniel of old. He and his brethren rejoiced that they were "counted worthy to suffer shame for his name. And daily in the temple, and in every house, they ceased not to teach and preach Jesus Christ." (Acts 5:41-42.)

As its prophet, seer, and revelator, Peter soon led the church into its boldest and most fruitful venture, fulfilling Jesus' commission to go "into all the world, and preach the gospel to every creature." (Mark 16:15.) In unhesitating response to divine manifestation, he opened the work of salvation to the Gentiles of every nation. "God is no respecter of persons," he declared to the converted Roman soldier, Cornelius, "but in every nation he that feareth him, and worketh righteousness, is accepted with him." (Acts 10:34-35.) When tradition-bound Jewish converts objected, Peter disarmingly replied, "What was I, that I could withstand God?" (Acts 11:17.)

Obedient to the principle that "unto whatsoever place ye cannot go ye shall send" (D&C 84:62), Peter wrote letters to the saints, at home and abroad. Two of these letters are included in the New Testament canon and contain what the Prophet Joseph Smith considered to be "the most sublime language of any of the apostles." (*History of the Church* 5:392.) Peter wrote of proper marriage bonds, of a royal priesthood, and of a good conscience. He encouraged charity, gracious hospitality, and escape from the pollutions of the world. He spoke of being born again and of a more sure word of prophecy. He bore witness of "the precious blood of Christ" and of the "divine nature" we all should desire. (See 1 and 2 Peter.) It is little wonder that so many then and so many now respond to Peter as did President Harold B. Lee. "[Often] when I want to pick up something that would give me some inspiring thoughts," President Lee once said, "I have gone back to the Epistles of Peter." (Message to Regional Representatives of the Twelve, April 1973.)

In a final moment of instruction before his ascension, Jesus had warned Peter of the course that lay before him. "When thou shalt be old, thou shalt stretch forth thy hands, and another shall gird thee, and carry thee whither thou wouldest not." (John 21:18.) That was, quite literally, part of what it meant for Peter to follow him. Christian tradition has suggested that Peter was executed by crucifixion but with his head downwards, lest he appear to be presuming in life or in death to be equal to the Savior he adored.

A recent announcement declared that excavations in Rome within the last decade had uncovered the remains of the apostle Peter. But Peter's bones were not discovered in that excavation nor will they be in any other, for the resurrected Peter appeared to the Prophet Joseph Smith on the banks of the Susquehanna River one hundred and forty-six years ago. On that sacred occasion the ancient First Presidency committed to Joseph Smith and Oliver Cowdery the keys of the Melchizedek Priesthood, which were to open a "dispensation of the gospel for the last times; and for the fulness of times." (D&C 27:12-13.) Through the mighty work of the Melchizedek Priesthood that has gone forth to all the world from that day to this, the "shadow of Peter" is still passing by and healing them, "every one."

9

Some Things We Have Learned—Together

Marriage is the highest and holiest of all human relationships—or at least it ought to be. It offers never-ending opportunities for the practice of every Christian virtue and for the demonstration of truly divine love. By the same token, marriage can also be the setting for struggle and difficulty, especially if husband and wife do not work as one. The following material is an attempt to discuss some aspects of that unity and is printed as it was originally given by my wife and me—together.

JEFF: This year we reach a milestone in our lives—we will have lived as long married to each other, twenty-two years, as we did before marriage. Surely that ought to justify some sort of sage advice from us. I was told on that fateful day in 1963 that with marriage I had come to the end of my troubles. I just didn't realize which end they were speaking of.

PAT: The last thing we want to do is sound self-righteous, so our first assurance is that our marriage is *not* perfect, and we have the scar tissue to prove it. To quote my father, the rocks in Jeff's head have not yet filled the holes in mine.

JEFF: So forgive us for using the only marriage we know, imperfect as it is, but for some time now we have wanted to reflect back on the half of our lives spent together since we were students at BYU and to see what, if anything, it might mean twenty-two years from now.

99

PAT: Let me reassure you that this isn't going to be the usual talk on matrimony. For one thing, we are going to try to apply these little lessons we have learned to everyone—single or married. For another thing, we fear that too many, especially women, are too anxious about the subject already. So please don't be anxious.

JEFF: On the other hand, I know a few men who ought to be a little more anxious than they are. Men, get anxious. Or to be slightly more scriptural, get "anxiously engaged."

PAT: We really believe that romance and marriage, if they are going to come, will come a lot more naturally if young people worry about them a lot less. By the same token, we also know that is easy to say and hard to do. It's hard because so much of our young life in the Church is measured on a precise time sequence. We are baptized at eight. At twelve the young men are ordained deacons and the young women enter Mutual. Then we date at sixteen, graduate from high school at eighteen, and go on missions at nineteen or twenty-one.

JEFF: But then, suddenly, it is less and less structured, less and less certain. When do we marry? Surely in a Church manual somewhere there must be a specific year for that! Well, there *isn't*. Matters of marriage are much more personal than a prepublished celestial calendar would allow. And so our anxiety level leaps.

PAT: With that acknowledgment, we are aware that some will not marry during their college years, nor perhaps during the years thereafter. By talking on this subject, we do not intend to make it more painful for some than it already is, but rather to draw some observations from our own marriage that might be of value to all—younger, older, married, or single. We pray for the blessings of the Lord to help us share something of our brief, ordinary, and sometimes tumultuous life together. *Another* twenty-two years of working things out would let us give a *much* better talk.

JEFF: With that long introduction, I don't know whether

this is our first piece of counsel or our last, but in any case, don't rush things needlessly and unnaturally. Nature has its rhythms and its harmonies. We would do well to fit ourselves as best we can *with* those cycles rather than frantically throwing ourselves against them.

PAT: As we look back on it now, twenty-two seems, if anything, pretty young to be getting married, though that was the right time for us. When it is right, it should be pursued, and for some that will be younger—or older—than others. But don't march to an arbitrary drummer who seems to be beating a frenzied cadence to the passing years.

JEFF: Twenty-one—

PAT: (Oh, dear, I'm facing . . .)

JEFF: Twenty-two—

PAT: (Will I ever find him?)

JEFF: Twenty-three—

PAT: (Oh, woe is me, woe is me.)

JEFF: Twenty-four—

PAT: (Death, make me thine! O grave, receive me!)

JEFF: Well, that's a little melodramatic, but not much.

PAT: We know of a few—not many, but a few—who have panicked that she . . .

JEFF: or he . . .

PAT: has not yet hit that matrimonial target established at ten years of age, or, worse yet, one established by a well-meaning aunt whose greeting every Christmas seems to be, "Well, you've been at BYU a full semester now. Have you found Mr. Right?"

JEFF: Or that solicitous uncle who says, "You've been home from your mission six weeks now. I guess wedding bells will be ringing soon, won't they? *They will, won't they?*"

PAT: Of course, we are not the best ones in the world to speak on that particular aspect, inasmuch as we were engaged thirty days after Jeff got home from his mission.

JEFF: Well, I had a solicitous uncle.

PAT: But you also have to remember that we knew each other well for two years before we started dating, dated another two years before Jeff's mission, and then wrote for those two years he was away. That's six years of friendship before we were engaged. Besides, when I first dated Jeff I couldn't stand him. (I just throw that in as reassurance to women who are dating men they can't stand.)

JEFF: I let her throw it in as reassurance to the men who can't be stood!

PAT: Then, still not to be outdone in the waiting game, I left for New York the day after we were engaged, leaving Jeff to hammer away at school while I studied music and filled a stake mission three-fourths of a continent away from him. That added another ten months, so I think it's fair to say we didn't rush things.

JEFF: Quite apart from the matter of school or missions or marriage or whatever, life ought to be enjoyed at every stage of our experience and should not be hurried and wrenched and truncated and torn to fit an unnatural schedule we have predetermined but that may not be the Lord's personal plan for us at all. As we look back today, we realize we have probably rushed too many things and been too anxious and too urgent for too much of our life, and perhaps you are already guilty of the same thing. We probably all get caught thinking real life is still ahead of us, still a little farther down the road.

PAT: Don't wait to live. Obviously, life for all of us began a long time ago—twenty-two years longer for us than for you—and the sand is falling through that hourglass as steadily as the sun rises and rivers run to the sea. Don't wait for life to gallop in and sweep you off your feet. It is a quieter, more pedestrian visitor than that. In a church that understands more about time and its relationship to eternity than any other, we of all people ought to savor every moment, ought to enjoy the time of preparation *before* marriage, filling it full of all the truly good

102

things of life—one of the most valuable of which is a university education.

JEFF: Let me add just one other related caution. In my professional and ecclesiastical life working with young adults—roughly the same second-half period of my life that corresponds to our marriage—I have regularly run into young men and women who are looking for that idealized partner who is some perfect amalgamation of virtues and characteristics seen in parents, loved ones, Church leaders, movie stars, sports heroes, political leaders, or any other wonderful men and women we may have known.

PAT: Certainly it is important to have thought through those qualities and attributes that you most admire in others, and that you yourself ought to be acquiring. But remember that when young people have visited with Sister Camilla Kimball about how wonderful it must be to be married to a prophet, she has said, "Yes, it is wonderful to be married to a prophet, but I didn't marry a prophet. I just married a returned missionary." Consider this statement from President Kimball on such down-to-earth choices:

JEFF: "Two people coming from different backgrounds soon learn after the ceremony is performed that stark reality must be faced. There is no longer a life of fantasy or of make-believe; we must come out of the clouds and put our feet firmly on the earth. . . .

"One comes to realize very soon after the marriage that the spouse has weaknesses not previously revealed or discovered. The virtues that were constantly magnified during courtship now grow relatively smaller, and the weaknesses that seemed so small and insignificant during courtship now grow to sizeable proportions. . . . Yet real, lasting happiness is possible. . . . [It] is within the reach of every couple, every person. 'Soulmates' are fiction and an illusion; and while every young man and young woman will seek with all diligence and prayerfulness to find a mate with whom life can be most compatible and beautiful, yet it is certain that almost any good man and any good woman can have happiness and a successful marriage if both are willing to pay the price." (*Marriage and Divorce*, Deseret Book, 1976, pp. 13, 18.)

PAT: On that note, let us share with you a little "stark reality" of our own. Jeff and I have conversations from time to time that bring us down "out of the clouds," to use President Kimball's phrase. Do you want to know what I have told him he does that irritates me the most? It is that he walks everywhere in a hurry—first five, then ten, then fifty feet in front of me. I have learned now to just call out and tell him to save me a place when he gets where he's going.

JEFF: Well, as long as we are telling secrets, do you want to know what irritates me? It is that she is always late and that we are therefore always running to get somewhere, with me first five, then ten, then fifty feet in front of her.

PAT: We have learned to laugh about that a little, and now compromise—I watch the time a bit better, he slows down a stride or two, and we actually touch fingertips about every other bounce.

JEFF: But we don't have everything worked out yet—like room temperatures. I used to joke about LDS scripturalists who worried about the body temperature of translated beings. I don't joke anymore, because I now worry seriously about my wife's body temperature. She has an electric blanket on high for eleven months of the year. She suffers hypothermia at the Fourth of July picnic. She thaws out from about 2:00 to 3:30 on the afternoon of August 12, then it's bundle-up time again.

PAT: He ought to talk. He throws the window open every night as if he's Admiral Peary looking for the North Pole. But just let someone suggest a little winter morning's jogging and he sounds like a wounded Siberian sheepdog. Mr. Health here can't tie his shoelaces without taking oxygen.

JEFF: As for different backgrounds, it's hard to think two

kids from St. George could have different backgrounds—or even any background at all. But regarding financial matters, Pat came from a family in which her father was very careful with money (and therefore always had some to share generously) while my dad grew up without any money but later spent it as generously as if he had. Both families were very happy, but when the two of us came together it was "Hail, Columbia . . ."

PAT: ". . . and the devil take the hindmost." That introduces to us another of those "stark realities" of marriage. To quote Elder Marvin J. Ashton in an address to the membership of the Church:

"How important are money management and finances in marriage and family affairs? Tremendously. The American Bar Association recently indicated that 89 percent of all divorces could be traced to quarrels and accusations over money. [Another study] estimated that 75 percent of all divorces result from clashes over finances. Some professional counselors indicated that four out of [every] five families [wrestle] with serious money problems. . . .

". . . A prospective wife could well concern herself not with the amount her husband-to-be can earn in a month, but rather how will he manage the money that comes into his hands. . . . A prospective husband who is engaged to a sweetheart who has everything would do well to take yet another look and see if she has money management sense." ("One for the Money," *Ensign,* July 1975, p. 72.)

Controlling your financial circumstances is another one of those "marriage skills"—and we put that in quotation marks—that obviously matters to everyone and matters *long* before entering into marriage. One of the great laws of heaven and earth is that your expenses need to be less than your income. You can reduce your anxiety and your pain and your early marital discord—indeed, you can reduce your *parents'* anxiety and pain and marital discord right now!—if you will learn to manage a budget.

JEFF: As part of this general financial caution, we encourage, if necessary, plastic surgery for both husband and wife. This is a very painless operation, and it may give you more self-esteem than a new nose job or a tummy tuck. Just cut up your credit cards. Unless you are prepared to use those cards under the strictest of conditions and restraints, you should not use them at all—at least not at 18 percent or 21 percent or 24 percent interest. No convenience known to modern man has so jeopardized the financial stability of a family—especially young struggling families—as has the ubiquitous credit card. "Don't leave home without it?" That's precisely why he is leaving home—

PAT: and why she is leaving him! May I paraphrase something President J. Reuben Clark said once in general conference:

"[Debt] never sleeps nor sickens nor dies; it never goes to the hospital; it works on Sundays and holidays; it never takes a vacation; . . . it is never laid off work . . . ; it buys no food; it wears no clothes; it is unhoused . . . ; it has neither weddings nor births nor deaths; it has no love, no sympathy; it is as hard and soulless as a granite cliff. Once in debt, [it] is your companion every minute of the day and night; you cannot shun it or slip away from it; you cannot dismiss it; . . . and whenever you get in its way or cross its course or fail to meet its demands, it crushes you." (*Conference Report,* April 1938, p. 103.)

JEFF: Your religion should protect you against immorality and violence and any number of other family tragedies that strike at marriages throughout the land. And if you will let it, your religion will protect you against financial despair as well. Pay your tithes and offerings first. No greater financial protection can be offered you. Then simply budget what is left the rest of that month. Make do with what you have. Do without. Say no. Your head can be held high even if your clothing is not the most stylish or your home the most regal. It can be held high for the simple reason that it is not bent or bowed with the relentless burden of debt.

PAT: Well, that's more than we intended to say about money, but we remember how it was when we were just starting out.

JEFF: I remember last month.

This last topic is the most difficult of all, and probably the most important. I hope we can communicate our feelings about it. Much has been said about the impropriety of intimacy before marriage. It is a message we hope you continue to hear often and one we hope you honor with the integrity expected of a Latter-day Saint man or woman. But now we wish to say something about intimacy *after* marriage, an intimacy that goes far beyond the physical relationship a married couple enjoy. Such an issue seems to us to be at the very heart of the true meaning of marriage.

PAT: Marriage is the highest and holiest and most sacred of human relationships. And because of that, it is the most intimate. When God brought Adam and Eve together before there was any death to separate them, he said, "Therefore shall a man leave his father and his mother, and shall cleave unto his wife: and they shall be one flesh." (Genesis 2:24.) To reinforce the imagery of that unity, the scriptures indicate that God had figuratively taken a rib from Adam's side to make Eve, not from his front that she should lead him and not from his back that she should despise him, but from his side, under his arm, close to his heart. There, bone of his bone and flesh of his flesh, husband and wife were to be united in every way, side by side. They were to give themselves totally to each other, and to "cleave unto [each other] and none else." (D&C 42:22.)

JEFF: To give ourselves so totally to another person is the most trusting and perhaps the most fateful step we take in life. It seems such a risk and such an act of faith. None of us moving toward the altar would seem to have the confidence to reveal *everything* that we are—all our hopes, all our fears, all our dreams, all our weaknesses—to another person. Safety and good sense and this world's experience suggest that we hang back a little, that we not wear our heart on our sleeve where it can so easily be hurt by one who knows so much about us. We fear, as Zechariah prophesied of Christ, that we will be "wounded in the house of [our] friends." (Zechariah 13:6.)

But no marriage is really worth the name, at least not in the sense that God expects us to be married, if we do not fully invest all that we have and all that we are in this other person who has been bound to us through the power of the holy priesthood. Only when we are willing to share life totally does God find us worthy to give life. Paul's analogy for this complete commitment was that of Christ and the church. Could Christ, even in his most vulnerable moments in Gethsemane or Calvary, hold back? In spite of what hurt might be in it, could he fail to give all that he was and all that he had for the salvation of his bride, his church, his followers—those who would take upon them his name even as in a marriage vow?

PAT: And by the same token, his church cannot be reluctant or apprehensive or doubtful in its commitment to him whose members we are. So, too, in a marriage. Christ and the church, the groom and the bride, the man and the woman must insist on the most complete union. Every mortal marriage is to recreate the ideal marriage sought by Adam and Eve, by Jehovah and the children of Israel. With no hanging back, "cleaving unto none other," each fragile human spirit is left naked, as it were, in the custody of its marriage partner, even as our first parents were in that beautiful garden setting. Surely that is a risk. Certainly it is an act of faith. But the risk is central to the meaning of the marriage, and the faith moves mountains and calms the turbulent sea.

JEFF: It would be well worth our time if we could impress upon you the sacred obligation a husband and wife have to each other when the fragility and vulnerability and delicacy of the partner's life is placed in the other's keeping. Pat and I have lived together for twenty-two years—roughly the time that each of us had lived alone prior to the wedding day. I may not know everything about her, but I know twenty-two years' worth, and she knows that much of me. I know her likes and dislikes, and she knows mine. I know her tastes and interests and hopes and dreams, and she knows mine. As our love has grown and our relationship matured, we have been increasingly open with each other about all of that for twenty-two years now, and the result is that I know much more clearly how to help her and I know exactly how to hurt her. I may not know all the buttons to push, but I know most of them. And surely God will hold me accountable for any pain I cause her by intentionally pushing the hurtful ones when she has been so trusting of me. To toy with such a sacred trust—her body, her spirit, and her eternal future—and exploit those for my gain, even if only emotional gain, should disqualify me to be her husband and ought to consign my miserable soul to hell. To be that selfish would mean that I am a legal, live-in roommate who shares her company but I am not her husband in any Christian sense of that word. I have not been as Christ is to the church. We would not be bone of one bone, and flesh of one flesh.

PAT: God expects a marriage, not just a temple-sanctioned understanding or arrangement or live-in wage earner or housekeeper. Surely everyone within the sound of my voice understands the severe judgment that comes upon such casual commitments before marriage. I believe there is an even more severe judgment upon me *after* marriage if all I do is share Jeff's bed and his work and his money, and, yes, even his children. It is not marriage unless we literally share each other, the good times and the bad, the sickness and the health, the life and the death. It is not marriage unless I am there for him whenever he needs me.

JEFF: You can't be a good wife or a good husband or a good roommate or a good Christian just when you "feel well." A student once walked into the office of Dean LeBaron Russell Briggs at Harvard and said he hadn't done his assignment because he hadn't felt well. Looking the student piercingly in the eye, Dean Briggs said, "Mr. Smith, I think in time you may perhaps find that most of the work in the world is done by people who aren't feeling very well." (Quoted by Vaughn J. Featherstone, "Self-Denial," *New Era*, November 1977, p. 9.) Of course some days are going to be more difficult than others, but if you leave the escape hatch in the airplane open because you think even before takeoff you might want to bail out in midflight, then I can promise you it's going to be a pretty chilly trip less than fifteen minutes after the plane leaves the ground. Close the door, strap on those seat belts, and give it full throttle. That's the only way to make a marriage fly.

PAT: Is it any wonder that we dress ourselves in white and go to the house of the Lord and kneel before God's administrators to pledge ourselves to each other with a confession of Christ's atonement? How else can we bring the strength of Christ to this union? How else can we bring his patience and his peace and his preparation? And above all, how else can we bring his permanence, his staying power? We must be bonded so tightly that *nothing* will separate us from the love of this man or this woman.

JEFF: In that regard we have the most reassuring of all final promises: *that power which binds us together in righteousness is greater than any force—any force—which might try to separate us.* That is the power of covenant theology and the power of priesthood ordinances. That is the power of the gospel of Jesus Christ.

PAT: May I share just one concluding experience that, although taken from our marriage, has application to you right now—young or old, married or single, new convert or long-time member.

110

Twenty-two years ago, Jeff and I, marriage certificate in hand, made our way to Brigham Young University. We put all that we owned in a secondhand Chevrolet and headed for Provo. We were not uneasy. We were not frightened. We were terrified. We were little hayseeds from St. George, Utah, and here we were in Provo—at Brigham Young University, where the world was to be our campus.

The housing people were very helpful in providing lists of apartments. The registration staff helped straighten out some transfer credits. The folks in the employment center suggested where we might work. We pieced together some furniture and found some friends. Then we splurged, left our new forty-five-dollar-a-month, two-room-and-a-shower apartment to have an evening meal in the Wilkinson Center cafeteria. We were impressed and exhilarated and still terrified.

JEFF: I remember one of those beautiful summer evenings walking up from our apartment on Third North and First East to the brow of the hill where the Maeser Building so majestically stands. Pat and I were arm in arm and very much in love, but school had not started, and there seemed to be so very much at stake. We were nameless, faceless, meaningless little undergraduates seeking our place in the sun. And we were newly married, each trusting our future so totally to the other, yet hardly aware of that at the time. I remember standing about halfway between the Maeser Building and the President's Home and being suddenly overwhelmed with the challenge I felt—new family, new life, new education, no money and no confidence. I remember turning to Pat and holding her in the beauty of that August evening and fighting back the tears. I asked, "Do you think we can do it? Do you think we can compete with all these people in all these buildings who know so much more than we do and are so able? Do you think we've made a mistake?" Then I said, "Do you think we should withdraw and go home?"

As a brief tribute to her in what has been a very personal

message anyway, I guess that was the first time I saw what I would see again and again and again in her—the love, the confidence, the staying power, the reassurance, the careful handling of my fears and the sensitive nurturing of my faith, especially faith in me. She (who must have been terrified herself, especially now, linked to me for life) set aside her own doubts, slammed shut the hatch on the airplane, and grabbed me by the safety belt. "Of course we can do it," she said. "Of course we're not going home." Then, standing there, almost literally in the evening shadows of a home we would much later, for a time, call our own, she gently reminded me that surely others were feeling the same thing, that what we had in our hearts was enough to get us through, that our Father in heaven would be helping.

PAT: If you stand on the south patio of the President's Home, you can see the spot where two vulnerable, frightened, newly married BYU students stood twenty-two years ago, fighting back the tears and facing the future with all the faith they could summon.

Some nights we stand and look out on that spot—usually nights when things have been a little challenging—and we remember those very special days.

Please don't feel you are the only ones who have ever been fearful or vulnerable or alone—before marriage or after. Everyone has, and from time to time perhaps everyone will yet be. Help each other. You don't have to be married to do that. Just be a friend, be a Latter-day Saint. And if you are married, no greater blessings can come to your union than some of the troubles and challenges you will face if you'll rev up your motor and bear straight ahead through lightning and thunder and turbulence and all.

JEFF: Paraphrasing James Thurber in one of the best and simplest definitions of love ever given, "Love is what you go through together." That counts not only for husbands and wives but also parents and children, brothers and sisters, roommates and friends, missionary companions, and every other human relationship worth enjoying.

Love, like individuals, is tested by the flame of adversity. If we are faithful and determined, it will temper and refine us, but it will not consume us. Enjoy what you now have. Be a disciple of Christ. Live worthily of marriage even if it doesn't come soon. And cherish it with all your heart when it does.

10

However Long and Hard
the Road

Often in our most difficult times the only thing we can do is endure. We may have no idea what the final cost in suffering or sacrifice may be, but we can vow never to give up. In doing so we will learn that there is no worthy task so great nor burden so heavy that will not yield to our perseverance. We can make it to "Mount Zion, . . . the city of the living God, the heavenly place, the holiest of all," however long and hard the road.

We speak about *excellence* a great deal these days, and, by definition, excellence does not come easily or quickly—an excellent education does not, a successful mission does not, a strong and loving marriage does not, rewarding personal relationships do not. It is simply a truism that nothing very valuable can come without significant sacrifice and effort and patience on our part. Many of the most hoped-for rewards in life can seem an awfully long time coming.

My concern is that we sometimes face delays and disappointments but feel that no one else in the history of mankind has ever had our problems or faced those difficulties. And when some of those challenges come, we will have the temptation to say, "This task is too hard. The burden is too heavy. The path is too long." And so we decide to quit, simply to give up.

To terminate certain kinds of tasks is not only acceptable but often very wise. If you are, for example, a flagpole sitter, then I say, "Come on down." But in life's most crucial and telling tasks, my plea is to stick with it, to persevere, to hang in and hang on, and to reap the reward. Or to be slightly more scriptural: "Wherefore, be not weary in well-doing, for ye are laying the foundation of a great work. And out of small things proceedeth that which is great. Behold, the Lord requireth the heart and a willing mind; and the willing and obedient shall eat the good of the land of Zion in these last days." (D&C 64:33-34.)

We must not give up, "for [we] are laying the foundation of a great work." That "great work" is ourselves—our lives, our future, the very fulfillment of our dreams. That "great work" is what, with effort and patience and God's help, we can become. When days are difficult or problems seem unending, we must stay in the harness and keep pulling. We are all entitled to "eat the good of the land of Zion in these last days," but it will require our heart and a willing mind. It will require that we stay at our post and keep trying.

On May 10, 1940, as the specter of Nazi infamy moved relentlessly toward the English Channel, Winston Leonard Spencer Churchill was summoned to the post of prime minister of England. He hastily formed a government and on May 13 went before the House of Commons with his maiden speech. He declared:

"I would say to the House, as I said to those who have joined this Government: 'I have nothing to offer but blood, toil, tears, and sweat.'

"We have before us an ordeal of the most grievous kind. We have before us many, many long months of struggle and of suffering. You ask what is our policy? I will say: It is to wage war, by sea, land, and air, with all our might and with all our strength that God can give us. . . . That is our policy. You ask, What is our aim? I can answer in one word: Victory—victory at all costs, victory in spite of all terror; victory, however long and hard the road may be." (*Churchill: The Life Triumphant,* American Heritage, 1965, p. 90.)

Six days later he went on radio to speak to the world at large. He said: "This is one of the most awe-striking periods in the long history of France and Britain. . . . Behind us . . . gather a group of shattered States and bludgeoned races: the Czechs, the Poles, the Norwegians, the Danes, the Dutch, the Belgians—upon all of whom the long night of barbarism will descend, unbroken even by a star of hope, unless we conquer, as conquer we must; as conquer we shall." (Churchill, p. 91.)

Then two weeks later he was back before Parliament. "We shall not flag or fail," he vowed. "We shall go on to the end, we shall fight in France, we shall fight on the seas and oceans, we shall fight with growing confidence and growing strength in the air, we shall defend our island, whatever the cost may be, we shall fight on the beaches, we shall fight on the landing grounds, we shall fight in the fields and in the streets, we shall fight in the hills; we shall never surrender." (Churchill, p. 91.)

I love these lines not only because they are among the most stirring calls to patriotism and courage ever uttered in the English language, but also because I relied on them personally at a crucial time in my life.

More than twenty years ago I stood on the famous white cliffs of Dover overlooking the English Channel, the very channel that twenty years before was the only barrier between Hitler and England's fall. In 1962 my mission was concluding, and I was concerned. My future seemed very dim and difficult. My parents were then serving a mission also, which meant I was going home to live I-did-not-quite-know-where and to pay my way I-did-not-quite-know-how. I had completed only one year of college, and I had no idea what to major in or where to seek my career. I knew I needed three more years for a baccalaureate degree and had the vague awareness that graduate school of some kind inevitably loomed up behind that.

I knew tuitions were high and jobs were scarce. And I knew there was an alarmingly wider war spreading in Southeast Asia, which could require my military service. I hoped to marry but wondered when—or if—that could be, at least under all these circumstances. My educational hopes seemed like a never-ending path into the unknown, and I had hardly begun.

So before heading home I stood one last time on the cliffs of the country I had come to love so much,

> This royal throne of kings, this scepter'd isle . . .
> This fortress built by Nature for herself
> Against infection and the hand of war.
> (*Richard II*, act 2, sc. 1, ll. 40-44.)

And there I read again, "We have before us many, many long months of struggle and suffering. What is our aim? . . . Victory—victory at all costs; victory in spite of all terror; victory, however long and hard the road may be. . . . Conquer we must; as conquer we shall. . . . We shall never surrender."

Blood? Toil? Tears? Sweat? Well, I figured I had as much of these as anyone, so I headed home to try. I was, in the parlance of the day, going to give it "my best shot," however feeble that might prove to be.

As we wage such personal wars, obviously part of the strength to "hang in there" comes from some glimpse, however faint and fleeting, of what the victory *can* be. It is as true now as when Solomon said it that "where there is no vision, the people perish." (Proverbs 29:18.) If our eyes are always on our shoelaces, if all we can see is this problem or that pain, this disappointment or that dilemma, then it really is quite easy to throw in the towel and stop the fight. But what if it is the fight of our life? Or more precisely, what if it is the fight *for* our life, our *eternal* life at that? What if beyond this problem or that pain, this disappointment or that dilemma, we really can see and can hope for all the best and right things that God has to

117

offer? Oh, it may be blurred a bit by the perspiration running into our eyes, and in a really difficult fight one of the eyes might even be closing a bit, but faintly, dimly, and ever so far away we can see the object of it all. And we say it is worth it, we do want it, we will fight on. Like Coriantumr, we will lean upon our sword to rest a while, then rise to fight again. (See Ether 15:24-30.)

But how, you ask, do we get this glimpse of the future that helps us to hang on? Well, for me that is one of the great gifts of the restored gospel of Jesus Christ. It is not insignificant that early in his life Joseph Smith was taught this lesson three times in the same night and once again the next morning. Moroni said, quoting the Lord verbatim as recorded by the prophet Joel: "I will pour out my spirit upon all flesh; and your sons and your daughters shall prophesy, your old men shall dream dreams, your young men shall see visions: and also upon the servants and upon the handmaids of those days will I pour out my spirit." (Joel 2:28-29.)

Dreaming dreams and seeing visions. The Lord's spirit upon all flesh—sons and daughters, old and young, servants and handmaidens. I may be wrong, but I can't imagine an Old Testament verse of any kind that could have helped this boy prophet more. He was being called into the battle of his life, for life itself, or at least for its real meaning and purpose. He would be driven and hunted and hounded. His enemies would rail and ridicule. He would see his children die and his land lost and his marriage tremble. He would languish in prison through a Missouri winter, and he would cry out toward the vault of heaven, "O God, where art thou? . . . How long. . . . O Lord, how long?" (D&C 121:1-3.) Finally he would walk the streets of his own city uncertain who, except for a precious few, were really friends or actually foes. And all that toil and trouble, pain and perspiration would end maliciously at Carthage—when there simply were finally more foes than friends.

Felled by balls fired from the door of the jail inside and one coming through the window from outside, he would fall dead into the hands of his murderers—thirty-eight years of age.

If all of this and so much more was to face the Prophet in such a troubled lifetime, and if he finally knew what fate awaited him in Carthage, as he surely did, why didn't he just quit somewhere along the way? Who needs it? Who needs the abuse and the persecution and the despair and death? It doesn't sound fun to me, so why not just zip shut the cover of your Triple Combination, hand in your Articles of Faith cards, and go home?

Why not? For the simple reason that he had dreamed dreams and seen visions. Through the blood and the toil and the tears and the sweat, he had seen the redemption of Israel. It was out there somewhere—dimly, distantly—but it was there. So he kept his shoulder to the wheel until God said his work was finished.

And what of the other Saints? What were they to do with a martyred prophet, a persecuted past, and a now hopeless future? With Joseph and Hyrum gone, shouldn't they just quietly slip away also—somewhere, anywhere? What is the use? They have run and run and run. They have wept and buried their dead. They have started over so many times their hands are bloodied and their hearts are bruised. In the name of sanity and safety and peace, why don't they just quit?

Well, it was those recurring dreams, and compelling visions. It was spiritual strength. It was the fulfillment they knew to be ahead, no matter how faint or far away.

In their very first general conference, convened three months after the Church was organized, the Saints had recorded this: "Much exhortation and instruction was given, and the Holy Ghost was poured out upon us in a miraculous manner—many of our number prophesied, whilst others had the heavens opened to their view. . . . The goodness and the condescension of a merciful God . . . create[d] within us a sensation of rapturous gratitude, and inspire[d] us with fresh zeal and energy, in the cause of truth." (*Times and Seasons* 4:23.)

There they were, approximately thirty members of the Church meeting in that tiny Peter Whitmer home in Fayette, planning to overthrow the prince of darkness and establish the kingdom of God in all the world. All the world? What presumption! Were they demented? Had they lost all power to reason? Thirty very average, garden-variety Latter-day Saints willing to work the rest of their lives? To what end? Persecution and pain and maybe thirty more members—for a grand total of sixty? Perhaps they did see how limited their immediate personal success would be, and maybe they even saw the trouble ahead, but they saw something more. It was all in that business of the influence of the Holy Ghost and heavens being opened to their view. President John Taylor said later of that experience: "A few men assembled in a log cabin; they saw visions of heaven, and gazed upon the eternal world; they looked through the rent vista of futurity, and beheld the glories of eternity; . . . they were laying the foundation of the salvation of this world." (*History of the Church* 6:295.)

Now there was to be a lot of bad road between the first conference of thirty people and a church that would one day have nations flocking to it. And, unless I miss my guess, there are several miles of bad road ahead of that church yet. But to have seen it and felt it and believed it kept them from growing "weary in well-doing," helped them believe even in the most difficult of times that "out of small things proceedeth that which is great." In a battle far more important than any battle of World War II would be, these Saints also vowed victory, however long and hard the road.

Though nothing in our lives seems to require the courage and patient longsuffering of those early Latter-day Saints, almost every worthwhile endeavor I can imagine takes something of that same determination. Even love at first sight—if there is such a thing—is nothing like love after some twenty years, if my marriage to Sister Holland is any indication. Indeed "the best is [always] yet to be." (Robert Browning, "Rabbi Ben Ezra.")

In that sense Troilus, whose impatient love for Cressida makes him something of a basket case, teaches us a valuable lesson. "He that will have a cake out of the wheat must tarry the grinding," Pandarus says to Troilus. "Have I not tarried?" Troilus pouts.

PANDARUS: Ay, the grinding; but you must tarry the bolting.
TROILUS: Have I not tarried?
PANDARUS: Ay, the bolting; but you must tarry the leavening.
TROILUS: Still have I tarried?
PANDARUS: Ay, to the leavening; but here's yet . . . the
        kneading, the making of the cake, the heating of the
        oven, and the baking; nay, you must stay the cooling too,
        or you may chance to burn your lips. (*Troilus and Cressida*,
        act 1, sc. 1, ll. 14ff.)

The baking of life's best cakes takes time. Don't despair of tarrying and trying. And don't "burn your lips" with impatience. Let me say just one bit more about the modern tragedy of sweethearts who will not tarry. It is of increasing alarm to me.

I do not speak here of specific lives or personal problems about which I know nothing and on which I would not pass judgment if I did. But the general matter of divorce, the abstract matter of divorce, is not only a major social but also a major symbolic problem in our world.

With the divorce rate hitting 50 percent and climbing, more than one million American children live through the trauma of a marital breakup every year. Andrew Cherlin of Johns Hopkins University says that "America[ns] . . . of the 70's and 80's are the first generation in the country's history who think divorce and separation are a normal part of family life." (Allan C. Brownfeld, "Who's Minding the Children," in *Divorce and Single-Parent Family Statistics,* p. 24.) That perception is being helped along by catchy new book titles like *Divorce, the New Freedom* and *Creative Divorce: A New Opportunity for Personal Growth.*

No one would wish a bad marriage on anyone. But where do we think "good marriages" come from? They don't spring full-blown from the head of Zeus any more than does a good education, or good home teaching, or a good symphony. Why should a marriage require fewer tears and less toil and shabbier commitment than your job or your clothes or your car?

Yet some couples spend less time on the quality and substance and purpose of their marriage—the highest, holiest culminating covenant we can make in this world—than they do in maintaining their '72 Datsun. And they break the hearts of many innocent people, including perhaps their own, if that marriage is then dissolved.

As President Spencer W. Kimball has counseled, we must not give half-hearted compliance to marriage. Marriage requires all of our consecration. (See Spencer W. Kimball, *Marriage,* Deseret Book, 1978, p. 10.) So every worthy task requires all that we can give to it. The Lord requires the heart and a willing mind if we are to eat the good of the land of Zion in the last days.

On July 28, 1847, four days after his arrival in that valley, Brigham Young stood upon the spot where now rises the magnificent Salt Lake Temple and exclaimed to his companions: "Here [we will build] the Temple of our God!" (James H. Anderson, "The Salt Lake Temple," *Contributor* 6 [April 1893]: 243.)

The temple, whose grounds would cover an eighth of a square mile, would be built to stand through eternity. Who cares about the money or stone or timber or glass or gold they didn't have? So what that seeds were not even planted and the Saints were yet without homes? Why worry that crickets would soon be coming—and so would the United States Army? The Saints just marched forth and broke ground for the most massive, permanent, inspiring edifice they could conceive. And they would spend forty years of their lives trying to complete it.

The work seemed ill-fated from the start. The excavation for the basement required trenches twenty feet wide and sixteen feet deep, much of it through solid gravel. Just digging for the foundation alone required nine thousand man days of labor. Surely someone must have said, "A temple would be fine, but do we really need one this big?" But they kept on digging. Maybe they believed they were "laying the foundation of a great work." In any case they worked on, "not weary in well-doing."

And through it all Brigham Young had dreamed the dream and seen the vision. With the excavation complete and the cornerstone ceremony concluded, he said to the Saints assembled: "I do not like to prophesy much, . . . but I will venture to guess that this day, and the work we have performed on it, will long be remembered by this people, and be sounded as with a trumpet's voice throughout the world. . . . Five years ago last July I was here, and saw in the spirit the Temple. [I stood] not ten feet from where we have laid the chief corner stone. I have not inquired what kind of a temple we should build. Why? Because it was [fully] represented before me. (Anderson, *Contributor*, pp. 257-58.)

But as Brigham Young also said, "We never began to build [any] temple without the bells of hell beginning to ring." (*Discourses of Brigham Young*, Deseret Book, 1973, p. 410.) No sooner was the foundation work finished than Albert Sidney Johnston and his United States troops set out for the Salt Lake Valley intent on war with "the Mormons." In response, President Young made elaborate plans to evacuate and, if necessary, destroy the entire city behind them. But what to do about the temple whose massive excavation was already completed and its 8' x 16' foundational walls firmly in place? They did the only thing they could do—they filled it all back in again. Every shovelful. All that soil and gravel that had been so painstakingly removed with those nine thousand man days of labor was filled back in. When they finished, those acres looked like nothing more interesting than a field that had been plowed up and left unplanted.

When the threat of war had been removed, the Saints returned to their homes and painfully worked again at uncovering the foundation and removing the material from the excavated basement structure. But then the apparent masochism of all this seemed most evident when not adobe or sandstone but massive granite boulders were selected for the basic construction material. And they were twenty miles away in Little Cottonwood Canyon. Furthermore the precise design and dimensions of every one of the thousands of stones to be used in that massive structure had to be marked out individually in the architect's office and shaped accordingly. This was a suffocatingly slow process. Just to put *one* layer of the six hundred hand-sketched, individually squared, and precisely cut stones around the building took nearly three years. That progress was so slow that virtually no one walking by the temple block could ever see any progress at all.

And, of course, getting the stone from mountain to city center was a nightmare. A canal on which to convey the stone was begun and a great deal of labor and money expended on it, but it was finally aborted. Other means were tried, but oxen proved to be the only viable means of transportation. In the 1860s and '70s always four and often six oxen in a team could be seen almost any working day of the year, toiling and tugging and struggling to pull from the quarry one monstrous block of granite, or at most two of medium size.

During that time, as if the United States Army hadn't been enough, the Saints had plenty of other interruptions. The arrival of the railroad pulled almost all of the working force off the temple for nearly three years, and twice grasshopper invasions sent the workers into full-time summer combat with the pests. By mid-1871, fully two decades and untold misery after it had been begun, the walls of the temple were barely visible above ground. Far more visible was the teamsters' route from Cottonwood, strewn with the wreckage of wagons—and dreams—unable to bear the load placed on them. The journals and histories of these teamsters are filled with accounts of broken axles, mud-mired animals, shattered sprockets, and shattered hopes. I do not have any evidence that these men swore, though surely they might have been seen turning a rather steely eye toward heaven. But they believed and kept pulling. And through all of this President Young seemed in no hurry. "The Temple will be built as soon as we are prepared to use it," he said. Indeed, his vision was so lofty and his hope so broad that right in the middle of this staggering effort requiring virtually all that the Saints could seem to bear, he announced the construction of the St. George, Manti, and Logan Temples.

"Can you accomplish the work, you Latter-day Saints of these several counties?" he asked. And then in his own inimitable way he answered: "Yes; that is a question I can answer readily. You are perfectly able to do it. The question is, have you the necessary faith? Have you sufficient of the Spirit of God in your hearts to say, yes, by the help of God our Father we will erect these buildings to his name? . . . Go to now, with your might and with your means and finish this Temple." (Anderson, *Contributor*, p. 267.)

So they squared their shoulders and stiffened their backs and went forward with their might.

When President Brigham Young died in 1877, the temple was still scarcely twenty feet above the ground. Ten years later, his successor, President John Taylor, and the temple's original architect, Truman O. Angell, were dead as well. The side walls were just up to the square. And now the infamous Edmunds-Tucker Act had already been passed by Congress disincorporating The Church of Jesus Christ of Latter-day Saints. One of the effects of this law was to put the Church into receivership, whereby the U.S. Marshal, under a court order, seized this temple the Saints had now spent just under forty years of their lives dreaming of, working for, and praying fervently to enjoy. To all appearances, the still unfinished but increasingly magnificent structure was to be wrested at this last hour from its rightful owners and put into the hands of aliens and enemies, the very group who had often boasted that the Latter-day Saints would never be permitted to finish the building. It seemed that those boasts were certain to be fulfilled. Schemes were immediately put forward to divert the intended use of the temple in ways that would desecrate its holy purpose and mock the staggering sacrifice of the Saints who had so faithfully tried to build it.

But God was with these modern children of Israel, as he always has been and always will be. They did all they could do and left the rest in his hands. Then the Red Sea parted before them, and they walked through on firm, dry ground. On April 6, 1893, the Saints as a body were nearly delirious. Now, finally, here in their own valley with their own hands they had cut out of the mountains a granite monument that was to mark, after all they had gone through, the safety of the Saints and the permanence of Christ's true church on earth for this one last dispensation. The central symbol of all that was the completed house of their God. The streets were literally jammed with people. Forty thousand of them fought their way on to the temple grounds. Ten thousand more, unable to gain entrance, scrambled to the tops of nearby buildings in hopes that some glimpse of the activities might be had.

Inside the Tabernacle President Wilford Woodruff, visibly moved by the significance of the moment, said: "If there is any scene on the face of this earth that will attract the attention of the God of heaven and the heavenly host, it is the one before us today—the assembling of this people, the shout of

'Hosanna!' the laying of the topstone of this Temple in honor to our God." (Anderson, *Contributor*, p. 270.) Then, moving outside, he laid the capstone in place exactly at high noon.

In the writing of one who was there, "The scene that followed is beyond the power of language to describe." Lorenzo Snow, beloved president of the Quorum of the Twelve Apostles, came forward leading forty thousand Latter-day Saints in the Hosanna Shout. Every hand held a handkerchief and every eye was filled with tears. One said the very "ground seemed to tremble with the volume of the sound" which echoed off the tops of the mountains. "A grander or more imposing spectacle than this ceremony of laying the Temple capstone is not recorded in history." (Anderson, *Contributor*, p. 273.) It was finally and forever finished.

The prestigious *Scientific American* referred to this majestic new edifice as a "monument to Mormon perseverance." And so it was. Blood, toil, tears, and sweat. The best things are always worth finishing. "Know ye not that ye are the temple of God?" (1 Corinthians 3:16.) Most assuredly we are. As long and laborious as the effort may seem, we must keep shaping and setting the stones that will make *our* accomplishments "a grand and imposing spectacle." We must take advantage of every opportunity to learn and grow, dream dreams and see visions, work toward their realization, wait patiently when we have no other choice, lean on our sword and rest a while, but get up and fight again. Perhaps we will not see the full meaning of our effort in our own lifetime. But our children will, or our children's children will, until finally we, with all of them, can give the Hosanna Shout.

God loves each of us and Jesus of Nazareth, his Only Begotten Son, came to "succor the weak, lift up the hands which hang down, and strengthen the feeble knees" (D&C 81:5)—bringing a divine form of worker's compensation to those who keep tugging those granite boulders into place. We are laying the foundation of a great work—our own inestimable future.

"Know ye not that ye are the temple of God?" Our life must be "a monument to Mormon perseverance," however long and hard the road.

Index

Shepherd, 21-22; is Lamb of
God, 22-23; is Prince of Peace,
23; is Stone of Israel, 23-24;
tempted by Satan, 27-28,
30-31, 33-34; member of body
of, 41-43; atoning power of, 79,
83-86; prepares Peter for
leadership of church, 91-95;
transfiguration of, 94;
relationship of, to Church as
model for marriage, 108-9
Johnson, Samuel, 57
Joy of repentance, 78, 86-88
Justice of God, 54-55

Kant, Immanuel, 46
Kelly, James, 37
Kennedy, John F, 2-3
Kimball, Camilla, 103
Kimball, Spencer W.: adversity of,
4-5; on call to apostleship,
31-33; fasting for, 50; on
forgiveness, 70; feelings of,
about Peter, 89-90; on Peter,
91-92, 96-97; on marriage,
103-4, 122
Knowledge, gospel gives, 48-49

Lamb of God, Christ is, 22-23
Lame, healing of the, 90-91
"Launch out into the deep," 92
Learning, example of, 60-61
Lee, Harold B., 48, 90-91, 98
Letters of Peter, 97-98
Lewis, C. S., 48, 56
Life, enjoying pace of, 100-103
Light and Life of world, Christ is,
21
Lincoln, Abraham, 47
Love, nature of, 47-48, 81-83,
112-13
Lucifer, 21

Macbeth, 68-70
"Man in the Water," 37-38
Marriage: Hollands use their
marriage to discuss, 99-101;
timing in pursuing, 101-3;
adjusting to, 103-5; financial
matters in, 105-7; intimacy in,
107-8; treatment of each other
in, 108-10; beginnings and
retrospect in, 111-13; and
divorce, 121-22; consecration
in, 122
Meetings, Church, 42-43
Membership, Church: feelings
concerning, 40-41, 51; as part
of body of Christ, 41-43; in
Teton Dam disaster, 43-44;
gives hope and comfort, 45-48;
benefits of, 48-50
Mercy, divine, 55-56, 85-86, 88
Messiah. *See* Jesus Christ
Mission call of Eli H. Pierce, 7-9
Missionary, Alma as, 87-88
Missionary Training Center,
example of missionary at, 66-68
Money, use of, 34-36, 105-7
Morality, 28-30
Moses, example of, 4-5
Muggeridge, Malcolm, 27-28

Names of Jesus Christ. *See* Jesus
Christ
Newlyweds, Hollands as, 111-12
Nibley, Hugh, 36
Noah, example of, 4

Omega, Christ is, 17-18

Pain of repentance, 78, 83-85
Pandarus, 121
Parents, efforts of, to teach
children, 81-82, 84-85